THE 21 LAWS
OF BEING AN
EXOTIC DANCER

Darius Allen has a degree in economics from the University of Southern California. He advocates that you should always visit a gentlemen's club with an agenda and a healthy attitude.

ALSO BY DARIUS ALLEN

The 21 Laws of Surviving a Gentlemen's Club

THE 21 LAWS
OF BEING AN
EXOTIC DANCER

Darius Allen

Varsity Club

PUBLISHED BY VARSITY CLUB PUBLISHING
a division of Varsity Club Enterprises, LLC.

www.varsityclubinc.com

Varsity Club

is a registered trademark of Varsity Club Enterprises, LLC.
Manufactured and printed in the United States of America
Library of Congress Cataloging in Publication Data

The 21 Laws of Being an Exotic Dancer/Darius Allen
1. Sex 2. Self-Help & Psychology
3. Women's Studies 4. Economics

Library of Congress Control Number: 2018901397

ISBN: 978-0-9974320-3-9

Cover design and Illustrations by Jesse Gonzales
Edited by Exotic Dancers

THIS BOOK IS DEDICATED TO YOU BRAVE SOULS WHO WORK THE POLE AND BARE IT ALL FOR THE ALMIGHTY DOLLAR.

YOU ARE APPRECIATED.

CONTENTS

Dancer's Note

Everyone can agree that the title "stripper" is the one that contains all the bite! Immediately, it triggers the imagination and spices up any dry, boring conversation. It's also more popular in use—thanks to hip-hop and its propensity to churn out strip club anthems like fast food; feeding an ever-growing strip club culture in cities like Houston and Atlanta. However, when choosing the official title for this book, the red light from the laser pointer had to be placed on the word *exotic*.

According to Merriam-Webster.com:

exotic

adjective ex·ot·ic \ig-ˈzä-tik\

1	: introduced from another country: not native to the place where found • *exotic* plants
2	*archaic*: FOREIGN, ALIEN
3	: strikingly, excitingly, or mysteriously different or unusual • *exotic* flavors
4	: of or relating to striptease • *exotic* dancing

No surprises there. Those definitions were to be expected and #4 does give a hint of life on the brass pole. But it's time to add a new multi-definition to the mix—from a jungle point of view, of course. The following acronym highlights the very reason for why this particular adjective is used to describe your type of dancing. Amid the loud music, the talkative DJ, the twerking, and the precipitation, this is what gets lost in (stripper) translation:

Enticing — to attract (someone) especially by offering or showing something that is appealing, interesting, etc.

X-rated — relating to or characterized by explicit sexual material or activity.

Open-minded — willing to consider different ideas or opinions.

Teasing — to arouse sexual desire in (someone) deliberately with no intentions of having sex.

Intoxicating — to excite or please (someone) in a way that suggests the effect of alcohol or a drug.

Captivating — to influence and dominate by some special charm, art, or trait and with an irresistible appeal.

To thrive in the jungle, you must embody what it means to be exotic. It's an essential quality that is necessary to create a strip club fantasy—not simply in looks and personality— that's a given. But you must embody for the patron what it means to be an exotic escape from reality; an exotic break from routine; an exotic creature that is sought-after lustfully with a thirst that is unquenchable in a world full of lookalikes and copycats.

Why else would a patron leave the outside world to enter your domain? There's plenty of women and entertainment options in the concrete jungle.

What does your jungle offer?

Being exotic is the major key that unlocks the game. Remember, you're an exotic dancer—not a *basic* dancer.

Preface

While writing *The 21 Laws of Surviving a Gentlemen's Club*, a group of dancers that were aware of the idea were hesitant to embrace it. On one hand, they had an undeniable curiosity about a book that dared to talk about the inner workings of the jungle. But on the other hand, an author who has the audacity to speak from a patron's point of view and stress a concept about surviving the jungle, had dancers back on their stripper heels. Survival? The patron? Are you serious?

Some of the fiercest dancers in the world were actually afraid that the book would create a campaign of marching strip club goers with picket signs chanting, "No More Rain! No More Rain!" Of course, that didn't happen, but they thought the purpose of the book was to knock their hustle and slow up their cash flow, not realizing that Law 16: Respect The Hustle—was strictly an endorsement of their profession and a salute to their "hustler" mentality.

If you digest the contents of *The 21 Laws of Surviving a Gentlemen's Club*, you will understand that one of the major themes of the book is the importance of the union between the Regular and the Favorite— it's the match made in strip club heaven. Not only does the entire industry exist because of this reciprocal, yin and yang relationship, but also, quite frankly, both sides need each other to coexist. Strip away the titles and break everything down to the nitty-gritty and seriously, what's an exotic dancer without a patron? And vice versa.

So, given that the first book dealt with patrons entering and surviving the jungle, it's only right to hear from those who have to work in the jungle.

Even though dancers were playfully referred to as predators (Tigers, Lions, Vultures, etc.) in the first installment of the 21 laws, everyone knows all too well that the true predator is the jungle itself. It gives no mercy and no preferential treatment to anyone—especially not to dancers. Despite their predatory instincts to hunt ballers and clean out simpletons on the main floor, dancers are still prey to the very nature of the industry.

There's only one law of the jungle—eat or be eaten.

Dealing with shady management, savage patrons, and backstabbing strippers on a nightly basis can have the most experienced dancers suffering from yellow fever.

With this project, several sharp and savvy dancers with colorful names (Nadia Ali, Dimples, Courtney, Nova, Honeydip2k, Egypt, Natasha, Jax, and Ayana), and from different backgrounds and locations (Los Angeles, Minnesota, Atlanta, Florida, Arizona, Houston, San Diego, Las Vegas) were consulted and conferred with about the goal of compiling 21 laws that will not only give aspiring dancers a rude awakening, but also give a behind the scenes look into a profession that has infiltrated the mainstream quicker than a hit song from Drake.

Forget Aquarius, we are living in the Age of the Stripper.

In these days and times, the spotlight on the stage is bigger than ever and the competition for well-paying patrons is at an all-time high. As strip clubs across the nation continue to reinvent the wheel and redefine themselves with several mirroring traditional nightclubs and sports bars, too many impressionable women are flooding the market, looking for a quick payday and a boost in social media followers. But in actuality, they are ushering in a new level of naiveté, recklessness, and unprofessionalism. As quoted by the great innovator and business titan, Henry Ford: "A market is never saturated with a good product, but it is very quickly saturated with a bad one."

Exotic dancers that are in touch with reality and hip to the game have to deal with this influx of newbies who only see dollar signs and not the warning signs. Their eyes light up when they see an OD (Original Dancer) collecting heavy rain and living a jet-setter lifestyle, and automatically assume that they can do the same.

"I mean…what's so hard about raking up a bunch of cash and partying every night? I can do that."

Not so fast. They don't realize that it takes a combination of emotional intelligence, sexual sophistication, and lady-like discipline to make a living in the chaotic, yet financially rewarding world of exotic dancing. One has to always be on their A-game. And the "A" doesn't stand for Ass. It stands for Adaptability.

So, while lawful patrons are busy endorsing their hierarchy of needs—the pyramid that represents the three main services that *only* a dancer can provide, and at the top is the coveted lap dance (see Fig. 1).

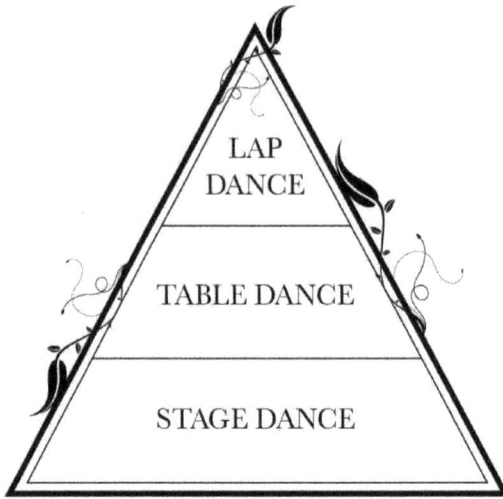

Fig. 1. Patron's Hierarchy of Needs.
From *The 21 Laws of Surviving a Gentlemen's Club* (p. 4),
2017, Varsity Club Publishing.

Exotic dancers have to constantly adapt to their environment, seize the moment, and keep their Stripper Money Cycle in constant motion, non-stop, with no brake pads or stop signs (see Fig. 2). This circular model identifies the three essential qualities that every exotic dancer must possess to not only make money on their shift, but to sustain a worthwhile career in the jungle. No dancer wants to hit the stage for mercy tips and empty compliments, and making the commitment to periodically enter the jungle and leave with little reward is heartbreaking. Money is the motive and this circle represents the eternalness of the strip club game.

Fig. 2. Stripper Money Cycle

SEX APPEAL

Regardless of a patron's individual taste and
preference—face, body type, style, and flavor—
every dancer must at least have some basic level of
sex appeal to even exist in the jungle. Sex appeal
allows one to enhance the fantasy, maintain the
mystery, and activate a boiling lust inside the most
reserved patron. The ability to break a neck, make a
heart pound with anxiety, and spark an uninhibited
imagination with thoughts of a one-night stand is
utterly priceless. This sex appeal is mainly expressed
visually (eye candy + stripper wear), but aura, body
language, smell, and vibes play a huge part.

HUSTLE

Hustle encompasses the daily "grind". Along with the job being a hustle (a side-hustle or full-time), to have hustle is to be in tune with the requirements of the job, be keenly aware of the importance of customer service and have a true understanding of the patron's hierarchy of needs. Whether providing a therapy session, a GFE, or a mind-blowing experience in a VIP booth, a positive and energetic attitude combined with an engaging personality and a relentless work ethic is a major key to success.

GAME

Game is the mental and physical chess match that is played with a patron to foster the relationship between the dancer's bag and the patron's money— turning a curious patron into a cherished Regular who spends "good money" is an essential part of the game. Within the rules of engagement, initiating a flirty conversation, whispering sweet nothings, and telling beautiful lies—along with the magical power of touch—are all strategic ways to keep the patron coming back again… and again…and again…

This Holy Trinity (Sex Appeal, Hustle, and Game) flows in unison and becomes one with the money. When all three qualities are clicking like clockwork—the money comes fast and consistent. In essence, time equals money. Not one second is wasted.

But if one or two aspects of the stripper money cycle slow down severely or take a significant hit, the dancer's staying power dwindles and spirals out of sync, running the risk of stripper stagnation: a prolonged period of making little to no money. A dancer can have **SEX APPEAL** that's off the charts, but without hustle and game, that sex appeal will flame out and become shallow. A dancer can out-**HUSTLE** her competition, but without sex appeal and game, that hustle will become routine and run stale. A dancer can have all the **GAME** in the world, but without hustle and sex appeal, that game will come off as manipulative and shady.

The goal is to always synchronize the three essential qualities. Like a hamster wheel, the cycle must be in a perpetual rotation at all times. It doesn't matter if you're working at a local spot hidden away in the Midwest, a buzzing gentlemen's club in the French Quarter in New Orleans, or a standing room only club in the jungle of all jungles: Las Vegas. You can be the best twerker in the world, an experienced therapist with a long list of clients, or a certified pole assassin:

The Stripper Money Cycle applies to every exotic dancer that is serious about securing a bag on a consistent basis.

If you want to make a living in the jungle, the cycle is the underlying source. Because once you're inside, deep in the trenches, working your tail off, you'll realize that there's no such thing as charity. Even donations come with the expectation of a return.

The 21 Laws of Being an Exotic Dancer is the sacred text that deals with the intricacies of a racy profession that is based on providing a sexual fantasy while being entrenched in a carnal reality. Few jobs (especially legal ones) require you to balance, contrast and merge the following dichotomies:

- **Business vs. Pleasure**
- **Predator vs. Prey**
- **Lies vs. Truth**
- **Fantasy vs. Reality**

Like a sexier version of Lady Justice, you preside over those dichotomies. In one hand, you're holding a scale, carefully weighing the benefits of each dichotomy, and in the other hand, you're armed with a sword, exercising judgment and cutting through the bullshit with swift force—minus the blindfold.

Normally, men are the ones at the roundtable creating laws and discussing their purpose, but this book breaks the mold and offers dancers the chance to discuss strategy and agenda on a familiar stage—the main stage.

Although this book contains humor, wordplay, and metaphors, by no means is this book meant for comic relief. Not securing a bag is no laughing matter. Similar to the jungle, this book is rough around the edges. It's harsh, provocative and direct—maybe too direct for some. But the kid gloves are off. This is as raw as it gets.

Laws 1-8: The Bare Necessities
◆ **Laws 9-13: Stripper Strategies**
◆ **Laws 14-15: The Sacred Union**
◆ **Laws 16-21: Main Floor Memoirs**

These 21 laws are the perfect counterpart to the patron's 21 laws. The conversation about life in the jungle continues. But don't get it twisted, this is not a battle of the sexes. That's what separates the 21 laws collection from the rest. This is more like a meeting of the minds with a little-added grind in the darkness of a VIP booth.

And you already know who's going to come out victorious.

Let's enter the jungle.

Introduction

Strong women wear their pain like stilettos. No
matter how much it hurts,
all you see is the beauty of it.

—Harriet Morgan

Talk to any OD (Original Dancer) who's
been knee-deep in the game, and she'll tell you that
being an exotic dancer is not for everyone. Strutting
gingerly on stage for the first time wearing a skimpy
fishnet outfit is an eye-opening experience. Not only
for thirsty patrons who are seated around the stage,
jokingly referred to as 'pervert row'. But for the
dancer, it's a self-revealing opening act that's often
met with uncertainty. Many think they're built for
the hustle, but once they're fully exposed, they
crumble right there in the middle of their second
song and start imagining life in a messy cubicle.

Unfortunately, the naked truth gets lost in
the outer beauty and allure of the jungle. So many
are fascinated by the "life" that they can't see past
the greenery and what truly lies beyond the surface.
All they see is the dollar signs and this leads to the
mythical belief that, in the jungle, money does grow
on trees. Combine that short-sighted belief with the

power of the almighty dollar and the influence of social media—along with rappers providing the soundtrack for the stripper lifestyle—exotic dancing has been and currently is the new wave. Simply put, a lot of women *want* to be strippers. They want the money and the attention, and they'd rather climb a pole instead of climbing a traditional job ladder.

Who wants to deal with a glass ceiling when you can use the ceiling as part of your pole performance?

In the blink of an eye, the profession has moved up the ranks from a "last resort" to a popular side hustle; a quick way to cash in on one's sex appeal while entertaining a herd of rainmakers. No longer is there a need to tell patrons that you're stripping to "pay tuition."

The word is out.

According to some dancers who happen to secure more bags than your local grocery bagger, the tables have turned. They're now the ones pointing the finger and laughing at civilians who are stuck working their 9-to-5s. They don't understand why these so-called "independent women" haven't escaped the corporate world to find a new place of refuge; the jungle. A place where there's enough rain to go around. And even if money doesn't grow on trees—money talks, and women who would never think of entering the jungle to dance are now starting to openly listen. The societal attitude towards those who twerk for a living has been rapidly changing its tune. Just take a look at the number of housewives that are taking pole dance classes. They're not shy about wanting to have a little taste of the strip club life. There is less public stigma and the taboo of sliding down a shiny pole is wearing off.

But it's still not for everyone.

For aspiring dancers, this is a hard pill to swallow. It's easier to ignore the pitfalls that are littered throughout the jungle. Regardless of the socio-economic reasons for this influx of Sapphires and Diamonds—whether it's the worship of strippers turned pseudo-celebrities, the popularity of reality television, or just pure "good old" self-preservation—behind the velvet curtain and underneath the thick skin of strong women who wear a different type of stiletto, is an undeniable struggle to handle the challenges of being an exotic dancer.

The decision to "flash for cash" takes real strength. Forget about the decision made by King James or any other person in the limelight—the decision to take one's talents to the jungle comes with pain that is seen and unseen. That decision may carry regrets, broken relationships, and personal shame.

You must ask yourself:

Do you have the strength to wear the pain?

That's the ultimate test.

Do not pray for an easy life in the jungle, pray for the strength to endure a difficult one.

But nowadays, with the focus only on money —mainly the beauty of it—the selfies with the racks of cash placed up to one's ear (money phone), the green carpet treatment on a bedroom floor, and the flashy videos of falling Benjamin Franklins, as well as the beautiful perks—courtside seats at the NBA game, backstage passes to the hottest hip-hop show, and a cell phone filled with talented photographers from Miami to L.A.—being an exotic dancer seems likes a painless walk-in the park; a peaceful twerk on a Sunday afternoon. Just another stop at the trap house on the way to the grocery store.

A few "stage dancers" will even try to convince you that working in the jungle is easy money. And you'll be a fool not to rush to the main stage like it's the California Gold Rush of 1849, not realizing that they're partly responsible for this oversaturation given the fact that they don't venture off into the dark and give lap dances. They conveniently leave that part out. But nonetheless, they will brag and tell you, "The money is falling from the sky and girl you better bring a bag. It's everywhere."

But behind the beauty of it all—is pain.

There is an old saying that applies to anyone in life looking for that shiny pot at the end of the rainbow—especially for those who want to enter the jungle and make a fortune.

All that glitters is not gold.

In this context, the glitter is the lustful but fleeting attention garnered by a sexy performance, the fickle popularity of having a strip club following, and the glamour of the fast life. The gold is a fool's gold of false expectations, mercy tips, and unlawful patrons who only want to demean the very person they come to visit: you.

In addition, while you're twerking and panning for gold, there's the mental and physical fatigue that comes from the daily grind of wearing the pain of an independent contractor. Without a doubt, you are on your own.

And that's only half of the story. There's the brutal competition between dancers; the same ones that smile in your face and ask to borrow your body spray, but behind your back, they can't wait to snatch up your Regulars.

Why do you think it's called the jungle?

Rarely does one on the hustle have time to take a seat on their favorite couch and give themselves a self-appointed therapy session and deal with the painful truth of being an exotic dancer.

This is where the 21 laws come in.

Instead of coping with the harsh reality of the strip club life with denial and suppression, and holding signs that cry out "Strippers Have Feelings

Too", these carefully curated laws will have you piercing through the jungle and cutting through the brush with a new sense of clarity and cunning. Being fluid and able to adapt to every encounter in the jungle—positive or negative—is the mark of a true professional. Staying focused in the midst of distractions and keeping your eyes on the prize (not the glitter) while maintaining your balance on the pole takes extreme discipline and perseverance.

If you're up to the challenge, you can find the strength to wear the pain and stake your claim in the jungle—not to be a plain Jane, not even to be a Queen—but to be a Jungle Goddess. To have an almost mythical quality to the levels of your seduction and femininity. When your every step can command an ATM withdrawal and a request for a scheduled appointment.

Simply adhere to the laws, use them as a framework and you will make more money, empower your volatile position, and be crowned an ATF (All Time Favorite) by all your Regulars—all the while avoiding the trappings of an environment that only wants to reduce you to just another stage name on the roll call.

Ultimately, you will accomplish your goal of exiting the jungle with your head up, heart intact (not completely frozen) and your bank account healthy enough to never look back.

THE 21 LAWS OF BEING AN EXOTIC DANCER

LAW

1

KNOW THE ENVIRONMENT

*In the struggle for survival, the fittest win out at the
expense of their rivals because they succeed in
adapting themselves best to their environment.*

—Charles Darwin

This law is strictly about awareness—a
heightened sense of awareness. To truly know the
environment is to know that you'll have to adapt
and survive a confined space governed by sexuality,
lust, and capitalism. You may envision a fun-filled
endless party with smiles and goodwill, but behind
the green door is a house of illusions; a hedonistic
entrapment full of beautiful lies and half-truths, not
to mention stereotypes and assumptions. As soon as

you find solace from dealing with all the stage names, fake personas, and masks, that's when you'll get blindsided by workplace favoritism and backroom politics. Nothing is above an environment that's vehemently driven by the *bottom* line.

First and foremost, it's a business. Period.

It's also a place where the overriding belief is that every dancer has a price—and when that number is called, you will gladly bow down to the power of the almighty dollar. Every tip is attached with a sneaky grin and a sinful request hoping that you're the one who's down to cross the line and engage in some extracurricular activity.

You're a book that will be judged by its cover.

And as you play the role of Jane of the Jungle, you're expected to know the ins and outs of an environment that rarely lends a helping hand. Before you can even think about your body getting "thicker"—you must first worry about having thick skin!

Ask yourself, "Do you *really* know the environment?"

Are you prepared to wander through the terrain on your own (topless or fully nude) with no Tarzan, no safari guide, and no treasure map? That's what it means to be an independent contractor. The onus is on you. No one can hold your hand and hustle for you. Consequently, while you treasure hunt for those bags full of money, hungry eyes will be glued to your every move, waiting for you to slip up and be at the mercy of the dollar bill.

The popular mantra is "money first" but it's actually safety first. You are the target. The bullseye is on your backside. And by no means is this a reference to a money gun or the loaded pistol that could be in a patron's pants during a steamy lap dance. That's low-hanging fruit; a basic talking point. This is about your state of mind and well-being. It's hard to exude sex appeal and secure a bag when you're fearful of being physically and verbally assaulted. Let alone the fact that your self-esteem will be under constant attack, steadily being poked in search of weakness and vulnerability. This environment is not for the weak-minded—that's a sure way to get eaten alive.

It's called the jungle for a reason.

And while some jungles are hole in the walls, resembling porn theaters of the 70s—make sure you bring holy water, disinfectant spray, and hand sanitizer—and others are lavish get-a-ways, something out of the esoteric movie, "Eyes Wide Shut"—never let the club's name, the decor and the spectacle of a flyer and a 30-second promo video distract you from what lies at the heart of every single jungle: **carnality**.

Understand that you're dealing with the lustful, animalistic side of human behavior—the lower self—a dangerous mix of ego, alcohol, and libido—and this carnal appetite for debauchery is expressed from both sides—male and female. You can take the most conservative, prudish woman in the world and throw her in the jungle, and an hour later, she'll feel compelled to grab some boobies and slap some ass. All of a sudden, she has a sense of entitlement, claiming ownership to every inch of your body. Her wondering eyes are now wondering hands, grabbing and squeezing, admiring every curve and beauty mark.

You are *her* plaything.

The next day, she will blame her behavior on the alcohol or claim to be possessed. But there's no such thing in the jungle.

It's simply the environment.

One that you'll have to navigate with your eyes wide open. Do not try to glamorize things by painting a pretty picture that doesn't exist. There's nothing high-brow about getting your G-string pulled by a drunken patron with beer breath. Having your butt cheeks grabbed by a group of rowdy patrons is nothing to write home about. Wiping down a dirty pole that's plastered in sticky sweat and body lotion is not a skill that you're dying to put on a one-page resume. Rubbing shoulders with flaky and untrustworthy dancers does not increase one's faith in friendships.

Too many become preoccupied with frivolous thoughts on how things *should be*, instead of dealing with *what is*.

You may think to yourself, "What's the big deal?" You get dressed up, you whisper into a patron's ear, twerk a lil' bit to your favorite song, and voilà! They turn into an ATM. Your bills get paid and you can continue living life as a bona fide shoeaholic.

Don't be naive.

Never underestimate the intensity of an environment that is inherently predatory. It feeds on your house fee and tip out, but it has a craving for your flesh. Your blood, sweat and tears is the main bulk of its diet. The environment can't function without you. It desperately needs you to exist. There is no strip club without the stripper. You are the source; the bloodstream that runs through the industry. Take yourself out of the equation, and the strip club quickly becomes an ordinary bar, a typical lounge, or better yet, a restaurant chain where the waitresses wear white tank tops and orange shorts.

But the cutthroat nature of the environment is to never let you know your true value. Often times, you'll find yourself fighting for attention that is rightfully yours. Nowadays, patrons and socialites are vying for the spotlight on stage and seeking their 15 minutes of strip club fame. In their minds, they are the life of the party and the night's entertainment—they're the ones on the flyer, right?

But never, ever forget the fact that you are the main attraction—not the Buffalo wings, the pepperoni pizza, the $2 steak special, the carne asada tacos, the hookah, the ballgame, and certainly not some random person hosting.

You are the money maker—the ultimate risk-taker, the hustler, the one that leaves it all on the stage. Your sanity and personal reputation is on the line.

Sadly, you're also the one that carries the burden of the industry. While staff and patrons are given a pass. All the stigma is placed upon your shoulders. The slander and shaming is directed towards you. In the span of one song, the spotlight from the stage can turn into a microscope where you're looked up and down extensively—and picked apart to the point of examination; from the tip of your toes to the top of your crown; from every tiger stripe and tattoo; to the way your fishnets squeeze and cuff your backside; and ultimately, to the speculative reasons on why you're on stage, spinning on a pole. You are on full display and the microscope is glaring and unforgiving. You will see a lot of smiles, but behind the scenes, you are treated like a pariah.

To a lot of shady managers, you're just another name on the roll call and some waitresses and bartenders will never fully submit to your higher-ranking position. They're too busy twerking instead of focusing on strip club hospitality. In defense, they'll tell you that it's all about the hustle, but deep down inside, they know that they're being parasitical and piggybacking off of your hustle.

#RespectTheStripper.

It's a cold game.

And it takes situational awareness to adapt to an environment that will drain you mentally and physically. It doesn't care about your feelings or your health. The pressure alone will cause a casual drinker to become an alcoholic overnight with a preference for brown liquor and tequila. The stress from the job might cause one to experiment with substances that would never have a chance of being in one's presence.

And here's the kicker, just when you think you've avoided those traps, you'll quickly forget that the environment itself is addictive. It has its own type of blue magic (100% pure dopamine). It gives you a heavy dose of lustful attention from men and women that will be overwhelming and difficult to manage, yet satisfying and alluring. Mix that with the thrill of the hunt, the paper chase and the adrenaline rush from receiving the green carpet treatment, and counting that money at the end of the night is a high that can only be reached again by another successful night on the job. You need another fix—asap! Hoping and praying that you experience another blockbuster "movie" night.

But the environment is unpredictable. The deep contrast between a Day-Shift and a Night-Shift is exemplary of the ups and downs, the highs and lows, the droughts and the rains storms that you will experience. The jungle can be jam-packed with investors throwing money everywhere and then, in one minute, it can turn into a ghost town. The only thing left is extreme boredom, empty tables and an urge to constantly check your cell phone.

Time can stand still or fly by with ease.

You'll never know what to expect. You can only learn to adapt without losing focus and purpose.

Because the daily grind will age you, adding bags under your eyes, and wrinkles from giving too many fake smiles. As far as experience, you will age in stripper years; 2 years of dancing is the equivalent of 6 years (multiply the year by 3). That calculation represents the strenuosity of an environment that will harden you and leave you with the impression that patrons are mere savages that only want to "eat, drink and be merry." Especially when you consider the cast of characters from all walks of life that frequent the jungle. From the Average Joe, the Gangster, the Nerd, the Girlfriend, the Pervert, the Stalker, the Party Animal, the Rookie, the Drug Dealer, the Lesbian, the Civilian, the Simpleton, the Married Man, the Couple, the Gentleman and the Regular—all in one room for a united cause—not for the Red Cross, the March of Dimes, or the YMCA—but for T and A.

Even Pimps slither their way through the club ready to unleash their verbal attacks (P-talkin) and offer their management services. Sidestep a Pimp's proposal, and you'll encounter a Shark who not only puts dollar bills in your G-string, but slides you a business card with a powerful title that comes with strings attached. For every Sugar Daddy that leaves a trail of sweets leading to a dark corner where you'll find a table and a cocktail, you'll meet a fuckboy with a pocket full of salt and a mouth full of disrespect. For every Whale that drowns you in dollar bills, you'll find a Cheapskate that never wants to tip but insist on groping you from head to toe.

Work at the right club, and you'll encounter superstar Athletes and Celebrities that will expect you to worship them while they try to finesse you and play on your insecurities. Right across the room, Strip Club Veterans and Rappers will want you to be an extra at their VIP table and a star in their home videos. And once every blue moon, you might see a Unicorn (Porn Star) make an appearance, suck the well dry and then disappear without a trace. Leaving you to pick up the scraps on the main floor.

The strip club environment is far from a walk in the park.

This all leads to one final question or maybe a stark warning. As you stand outside the jungle and look up at the marquee.

Are you still sure you want to be an exotic dancer?

Think long and hard.

If so, be ready for an environment that thrives on keeping you in the dark and on your toes.

DANCER NOTE

Your first step can't be a misstep. You have to know what you're getting into mentally and physically. The jungle is an intense environment that forces you to constantly adapt and straddle a thin line between sexual chaos and order.

LAW
2

CHECK YOUR BAGGAGE AT THE
DOOR

It's freeing to not be caught up in your own personal
baggage.

—Diane Paulus

As you walk into work with your signature bag strapped around your shoulder, passing bouncers and staff, it is important that you treat your entrance as a ceremonious event. It's not just a random, casual walk-in. You have a scheduled appointment with the stage and you mean business. For all intents and purposes, your *catwalk* into the jungle is a mental exercise that is methodical and ritualistic. You are walking the green mile. With every step, you are clearing your head, mentally preparing to enter your one and only sanctuary: the dressing room.

Before hitting the main floor and getting to that bag, you must first cleanse your mind of any negative energy.

It's time to examine your baggage.

Inside your bag, should be only sexy outfits, a few good luck charms to summon the Stripper Gods, a mesmerizing fragrance, a money bag, all sorts of toiletries (feminine products), a small stripper care package (candy & snacks), pole dance grip, and if need be, enough makeup to do a YouTube tutorial—basically your typical bare necessities for the job.

If times are rough and you're experiencing a drought, some rosary beads and a Ouija board are few exceptions. But any extra baggage as in your emotional and financial insecurities, family issues, and current relationship drama—especially problems with the baby daddy—should be identified and immediately checked at the door. Tag 'em and toss 'em to the side. Leave them right there at the entrance. That means whatever drama and stress you are dealing with in the outside world, do not dare bring that negative energy into your place of work.

Now, exercising this law is easier said than done. Life is full of challenges and setbacks that will make you want to stay in bed with a cold pillow instead of going to work and twerking up a storm. It doesn't take much for one to get knocked off track. One simple text message can severely dampen your spirits and put you in a miserable mood. It comes with the territory of being a human being living in this crazy world. But to be a professional, an exotic dancer whose eyes are on the prize, is to know that there is a time and place to deal with those issues and the jungle is not the right environment. Being a bag lady and carrying those burdens with you is counterproductive to your money-centric agenda. The goal is to create a strip club fantasy, not an ongoing nightmare. You have to be extremely focused and optimistic to secure a bag and those extra items add zero value to your presence and overall performance. They are literally and figuratively dead weight that slow down the rotation of your stripper money cycle (Sex Appeal, Hustle, and Game).

If you decide to bring that extra baggage into the jungle, at some point you will feel the urge to open up them up and reveal the contents. This is a crucial mistake. You may think it's cute to talk about your personal problems and spill some of your tea, but it's problematic and volatile. Exposing your private dealings will only complicate things and bring more stress and confusion to issues that need clarity and perspective. Especially when you share them with nosey dancers who can't wait to

add their misguided opinions and hasty advice—
which is inevitable. So many dancers love to gossip
and stir up chaos, adding fuel to any fire that they
can find in the jungle.

In a social environment that naturally pushes
your buttons and pulls on your G-string, you must
protect your energy and manage your emotions at
all times. Possessing emotional intelligence is the
ability to identity your feelings and show
discernment.

How does your emotional state apply and
improve your agenda?

Never forget that a strip club is a place for
escapism and you are a major part of that overall
escapism. For most patrons, it's a temporary hideout
from responsibilities and the hardships of life. They
pay a cover to experience a much-needed break
from the negativity of the outside world. Initiating a
lighthearted conversation about life and purposely
telling a sob story is strategically one thing, but
becoming the grumpy and bitter stripper who wants
to dump their baggage on a patron's lap is another.
No one enters the jungle to pop bottles and make it
rain on Debbie Downer and Negative Nancy—
regardless of how good you look. Don't be misled by
a few simpletons that enjoy hearing you at your
worst and tolerating any type of gloomy behavior.
Those type of patrons do not sharpen your game

and improve your hustle. Like a Sugar Daddy, they're looking for an opportunity to offer solutions to your problems and fill a void. But the average patron who consistently spends money comes to the club to escape drama, not to encounter it. And nothing ruins a fantasy like a heavy dose of depressing reality. That negative energy is a dark cloud that produces no rain. It also has other damaging side-effects:

Negative energy will have you subconsciously downplaying your skills and appearance. The entire room can sense your lack of confidence. Your swagger is off and your sex appeal is running on empty. Your eye contact and body language scream that you'd rather be anywhere else besides the strip club.

Negative energy can attract the most unlawful patrons who can't wait to dump their extra baggage on you. Misery loves company, especially in a strip club. And it's never the type of company that you want to entertain or turn into a Regular.

Negative energy will make you irritable and prone to complaining about the ills of the strip club life, instead of taking advantage of your time and focusing on your bag. Time is money, but that's forgotten while you're on your cell phone texting a friend about how life sucks.

Negative energy can run off a patron who's looking to spend a pretty penny on a therapy session. He's looking for some relationship advice and a shoulder to cry on, but you're too busy dealing with the chip on *your* shoulder.

Negative energy will affect your stage performance. Air walking on a pole is instantly seductive and captivating but not when it's done with a resting bitch face. It's hard to garner tips when you look severely bothered and unenthused during your showcase. Should you receive tips for frowning and mean mugging?

Negative energy can have you overacting to an innocent comment made by a dancer whose intentions were not to cause any type of drama. Before you know it, you have started a long-standing beef over nothing and everyone has taken sides.

And those examples above highlight the importance of the **Dressing Room**. In the jungle, the dressing room is your temple. It is your one and only sanctuary—treat it as such. It is a sacred place that provides you the opportunity for personal space and mental preparation.

Negative energies can't touch you if you are in a state of meditativeness.

—Sadhguru

Amidst the idle chatter and the back and forth yelling, you can take a deep breath, put your items on the table and truly get your mind right. Let go of any negative energy.

Do not take the dressing room for granted. It's a reserved area for a reason. It's far more than a room filled with high school gym lockers and annoying signs displaying the strict house rules. This is *your* room.

No patron can enter and, for the most parts, managers and staff keep a healthy, respectful distance. You are conveniently tucked away safely from the savagery on the main floor.

Unfortunately, too many dancers view the dressing room as a battleground; they only see it as a crowded sorority house (Alpha Delta Drama) full of clashing egos and stare downs. A place where dancers constantly size each other up and try to spot the weakest link. Instead of entering the dressing room drama-free and respecting everyone's privacy, some dancers like to bring in their extra baggage and find issue with the fact that there's no vacant space for their unwanted belongings.

Consequently, this is why 99.9% of fights happen in the dressing room. Its true purpose gets lost in vents of frustration and gossipy disputes. Disagreements happen, emotions escalate and things boil over. Next thing you know, there's a tussle and cell phones are pulled out, recording the melee. And within seconds, it's plastered on certain media outlets like WorldStarHipHop and The ShadeRoom for Dancers— #TheDancerLockerRoom. It's utterly embarrassing. On top of that, some use the dressing room as a ripe opportunity to become a cat burglar and get a case of the sticky fingers. Turn your head for one second, and makeup and money disappear like a magic trick. It's one of the most disheartening experiences that you can face in the jungle. It happens so much that some dancers should change their stage name to Klepto. When the DJ announces a 2 for 1 special, they're thinking about all the little items they can stash away in their bag.

To be clear, thievery is a pure violation of the 21 laws. But if you know the environment, you know that you have to watch your surroundings and never be caught off guard.

Do not succumb to the temptation of underutilizing your private sanctuary. If any type of stripper sisterhood exists, the dressing room would be the origin of that shared solidarity. This is where strippers hold hands and say their prayers, and hope for rain and blessings from the Stripper Gods. It's also the ideal location for bonding and healthy dialogue about the job and the industry.

OBSERVATION. Be careful not to expose too much of the activity that goes on in the dressing room. Some things need to be sacred. With the popularity of social media, a lot of dancers are using the dressing room as a location in their Stripper Reality Show. They are "going live" and interacting with their followers and using video as a form of marketing—and a way to pass the time. It makes sense. You're advertising your brand. But keep in mind, some dancers relish their privacy and would rather not spend their time ducking and dodging your pictures and video footage. Not every dancer is trying to be seen or captured on video while they're getting dressed or undressed. Be considerate and thoughtful of those who want to enjoy their personal space.

DANCER NOTE

The jungle is a place for escapism and bringing in your negative vibes has a negative effect on your agenda. How do you expect to secure a bag when you're too busy carrying extra baggage and worrying about its contents?

LAW

3

ALWAYS CREATE A COMPELLING

VISUAL

*For me, visuals are as important as the music. I just
love escapism and giving people something to
escape to. To me, that's what art is.*

—Iggy Azalea

While fiddling through your bag, deciding
on the perfect outfit that you think will slay the
competition, take a serious moment to think to
yourself: The multibillion-dollar strip club industry
is fueled by the simple fact that men are visual
creatures.

It's a craving that rarely gets satisfied.

Add women to the mix, and the spotlight becomes bigger, but at the same time, microscopic. Women are more critical about your presentation than men. They focus on the details, catching the little things that a salivating male patron will surely miss. But regardless of what side of the fence the patron is on, everyone likes a nice piece of eye candy.

With money on the line and competition at your heels, it's vital that you **invest** in your appearance and feel free to express yourself in an environment that begs you to be eye-catching—you gotta pay to play. Even if you work at a club that has ridiculous rules on what you have to wear (pasties, liquid latex, 2 pairs of underwear, nipple tape, etc.) and how sexy you can be (no girl on girl acts, no nipple licking and humping), you're still expected to find a way to turn heads. No matter how much those rules hinder your creativity, those expectations never go away.

You have no excuses and the pressure is on.

Just because men are visual creatures with an insatiable appetite for lust, it doesn't mean that they lack standards. Best believe that men are aware of their options and they're not hesitant to explore them. When a patron decides to enter the jungle, they've weighed their options and made a sound decision. Keep in mind, that you are competing with the following:

The Internet (pornography & cam girls).
Eye-candy on social media.
Digital and print magazines.
Nightclubs and bars.
Escorts and prostitutes.
And soon, very soon, you will be competing with sex dolls, sexbots and virtual reality.

So, again, why should a patron enter the jungle and spend their hard-earned money on you? What makes you stand out?

It all starts with the visuals. Remember, you're an exotic dancer. You're not a basic dancer, not a familiar dancer, not a typical dancer and certainly not an ordinary dancer.

THE BASICS

Smile. First and foremost, take heed of this priceless quote from actress Connie Stevens:

"Nothing you wear is more important than your smile."

Although she probably wasn't thinking about the jungle, that doesn't mean you shouldn't treat this quote as strip club gospel. She is 1000% correct. Delivering a natural, genuine smile is like striking a patron with a bolt of lightning. It can render the most protective, arrogant patron defenseless. It can freeze time and bring comfort to those in need of a therapy session. Or those that need a break from the harshness of reality. A smile is also the perfect trap that can get the attention of any type of patron. Flash a killer smile and let the games begin.

Stripper Wear. One of the key components of a strip club fantasy. The right outfit can turn a patron into an investor in seconds. That's why your bag should be filled with leggings, teddies, micro skirts, fishnets, lingerie, bodysuits, G-strings, thongs, and swimsuits—and that's just one bag. You can fill an entire closet with stripper wear. And, of course, if you want to make a lasting impression, you can always wear your Birthday suit. But whatever outfit you choose, make sure the color pops and it fits your body type. There's no reason to work against yourself. Always rely on the old adage "Wear the stripper clothes, don't let the stripper clothes wear you."

Stripper Shoes. Take your pick. You can roam the main floor in rhinestone stilettos or you can conquer the stage in ankle boots covered in rainbow fringe. You've got platform slides, strapped sandals, knee-high boots, slip ons, and if you want to send a clear message, you can wear some clear heels with the money in the bottom. With so many eccentric styles and colors, you have no excuse not to find a pair that can accentuate your best qualities and show a little personality. The right pair of shoes puts that extra arch on your backside.

Warning: Pick the wrong pair and you will be wearing your pain. The next thing you know, you're learning the tricks of the trade from an OD who's saying that you should have blow-dried the clear plastic on your heels to loosen them up. No one said it was gonna be easy.

Hairstyles. Unlike corporate America, the jungle (most of them) welcomes all types of hairstyles. Do you want to wear braids? Pigtails? Go ahead. Buzz cut? No issue. Whatever hairstyle you choose, make sure it taps into your alter-ego. Also, keep in mind that if you're on the hustle, chasing that bag things will get sweaty. So pick a style that can handle the grind.

Toes: A nicely done pedicure from your favorite nail lady does wonders for your self-esteem and sex appeal. Instantly, you feel complete and ready to conquer the jungle. Everyone can see it on your face. But this is about much more than having pretty feet with cotton candy pink polish. Do you know how many patrons have a foot fetish? No, seriously. Do you know? This might not be your favorite topic to discuss. In fact, so many shy away from a conversation dealing with feet. Just know there's a secret society of foot lovers and the majority of them frequent the strip club scene.

ACCESSORIES

Pasties. If you work at a club that doesn't allow you to free the nipple, but they don't limit your creativity beyond the typical "X marks the spot, " then luckily, you have a wide variety of pasties to choose from. You can take things back to Art Class and pick your favorite pasties covered in glitter, rhinestones, and sequins. It's all about the details. This is an accessory that is the equivalent of putting the cherry on top of the ice cream sundae.

Nose Rings/Piercings. Do you.

Stripper Glitter. Use at your own risk. Things can get messy, especially on a pair of jeans.

Tooth Gems. Yes, yes, yes. Very few things compliment a genuine smile like the bling of a tooth gem. It's the icing on the cake; a unique flair that can shine brightly in the dark. Keep it creative and fun. Why settle for an ordinary smile, when you can have a fly smile?

Tiger Stripes. Wear them proudly. Period.

Earrings. Keep it fun and glamorous.

Ear Piercings. Do you.

Makeup. This is up to you. If makeup is not your thing, it's not your thing. A thirsty patron won't turn down an amazing time just because your makeup isn't caked on. But if you do choose to put on some makeup, there's nothing wrong with slaying the competition and forcing every dancer to ask you for pointers and what's hidden in your cosmetics bag. When in doubt, here are a couple of winning combinations that are sure to create a compelling visual:

> *Soft Smokey Eyes + Nude Lips.*
> *Pinkish or Burgundy Lips + Simple Eyes.*
> *Contoured Face with Blush + Bronze Finish + Neutral Lips and Eyes.*
> *Dramatic-winged Tip Eye Liner + Red Lips.*

Side note: When it comes to your **Brows** and **Lashes**—Thou Shalt Always Slay!

Wigs. If you work at a club that understands the power of role play and doesn't mind letting their dancers think outside the box, wigs are an amazing tool that allows you to tap into various alter-egos and personas. You can play around with your multiple stage names and bring out different looks and characters that enhance the fantasy and make the strip club experience truly unforgettable. Just watch the expression on your Regular's face as you approach with a whole new identity and swagger. You'll find yourself in a VIP booth in no time.

MIND FUCKS

Pubic Hairstyles. There are eye-catchers and then there are eye-openers. The landing strip is a popular way to keep a patron's eyes on the runway and their dollars bills ready to land into your bag. It also doesn't limit the type of outfits you can wear. The versatility of the landing strip is unmatched.

If you want to make a scene and be at one with the jungle, then you can have a full bush on display for any and everyone to see. Talk about creating a compelling visual. But don't be surprised if most patrons stop what they're doing and spit out their drinks. The full bush can create mass hysteria. You can always go Brazilian and leave your pubic hairs completely out of the equation. You'll give a new twist to the term "Baby Stripper." Now, if you want to have a little hair present, then getting a bikini line trim is a little bit more mature. But whatever you decide, make sure you feel comfortable with your decision.

Tongue Piercings. This is a no-brainer. Flashing a tongue piercing wakes up any patron that's caught dozing off in the jungle. It's an eye-catcher that provokes fantasies about fellatio and all sorts of tongue play. There's no way around it. It does what it does. That's why it's not encouraged in corporate America. Can you imagine having a serious business meeting and your partner is making sure their tongue ring is visible to the entire room? It's a mind fuck and a distractor that hits the bullseye every time. Luckily for you, that type of distraction centers around you and your agenda.

Nipple Piercings. These piercings have a magnetic attraction that keep a patron's eyes glued to your chest. They can't help but notice these eye-catchers as they try their best to strike up a serious conversation. Especially if you have big breasts that basically slap them in the face. Not only do they signal that you enjoy a rush of pain, but they show that you focus on pleasurable sensations.

Similar to a hypnotist swinging a clock, nipple piercings allow you the opportunity to stir the conversation in whatever direction you want.

Vaginal Piercings. Nothing can stop a patron in their tracks like the sighting of a piercing located below the bush. Instantly, the topic changes to sex and the reasons behind your erotic piercing. You'll be answering questions for the whole shift. It also triggers a patron's imagination with fantasies of cunnilingus and other types of sexual stimulation, which is a blatant reminder that they're stuck in a fantasyland. The vaginal piercing is the ultimate example of "you can look, but don't touch."

WEAPONS

Tattoos. These works of art are natural eye-catchers and inside the jungle, every single one can be displayed without stigma and shame. A dancer is totally free to let those butterfly wings on her butt cheeks flutter around and admire the environment. If you're a dancer that loves the ink lifestyle—addicted to the needle—you can conveniently use your tattoos as a conversation starter, or better yet, as sexual bait leading a patron into a dark VIP room. They are the perfect lure that never fail to grab attention and induce intrigue. Especially when your tattoo is located in the right spot. It sends an encrypted message shrouded in lust and suggestiveness. There's nothing like a dragon on your back or a leopard print on the side of your torso to signify that a wild time awaits. If you want to start some trouble, flash that fully loaded pistol on the front of your thigh and then ask the patron if they can relate.

Nails. In the creative world of stripper nails (coffin, almond, and stiletto), you can literally have a set of flashy claws that will keep a patron in your clutches or you can get a nice set of shark teeth that can sink into a whale's pockets. With an endless variety of color schemes and styles—don't forget the ever-popular French manicure—you can blind your prey with a bedazzled set of nails as you slowly grace their neck, awakening their goosebumps. Through self-expression, your nails are a convenient weapon for seduction and attraction.

Side note: Chipped nail polish is never an option.

Scent. Although a scent is not a piece of clothing, it's still something that you wear. Similar to a smile, a scent is instantly persuasive. And every dancer who's spent time in VIP with a patron knows the power of a seductive scent. Whether it's from a body spray, perfume, body splash, lotion, or one's natural pheromones, this so-called "stripper smell" can send a patron into a dream state. Especially if you pick the right scent that can create a déjà vu type of scenario. That's when a patron has a flashback to an amazing time in their life when they were floating on cloud 9. If you can create that feeling, then you know you have a powerful scent.

OBSERVATION. There's one specific day that is highly celebrated and tailor-made for you to create a compelling visual. It was brought to life in *The 21 Laws of Surviving a Gentlemen's Club.*

Law 20: The Only True Special Event Is
Halloween.

On that spooky day, you can give all your Tricks a

nice Treat. The moonlight is on you and you can have some freaky fun with your alter-ego, wearing the Halloween costume of your choice. Creatively, you can be whoever you want; a sexy Librarian, a Mermaid, a Nurse, an Egyptian Goddess, a Cat Woman, a Cougar, a Vampire, a Ninja, the list goes on and on. Add in some role-play and timely Halloween-themed music and the jungle turns into a haunted house with body snatchers everywhere. Just make sure you take your bodies to the VIP room.

WHAT ABOUT PLASTIC SURGERY, ASS SHOTS AND OTHER COSMETIC PROCEDURES?

In the jungle, you can see some of the most perfectly shaped bodies in the world, thanks to hard work, a trendy diet, and a personal trainer—and for some, a reputable plastic surgeon. And then you can see some things that'll make you want to scratch your head. There's no need to put anyone on blast, but it's quite evident that some dancers have taken this law and pushed it to a whole new level. Unfortunately, to the point of no return.

The desire to secure a heftier bag has dancers from everywhere saving up their money to get "work done." Sabbaticals are taken daily. A few are even hitting up their sponsors and having them cover the expenses. As a natural body becomes more and more rare, the once difficult decision is becoming as normal as selecting what type of fishnets to wear. It's an everyday topic. And given that dancers are the sexier version of Lady Justice, the pros and cons are weighed daily and judgment is swift and subjective.

The question is, how far are you willing to go to create a compelling visual?

Let's examine the philosophy behind this new industry standard.

Does the average patron salivate over a ridiculous set of big boobs and an eye-watering, curvy ass? Yes. Can you work in the jungle, provide sexy visuals, and make a lot of money without a huge set of big boobs and a curvy ass? YES! Without a doubt, you can. And there's plenty of dancers who are representing #TeamNatural, #SmallButtsMatter, and #RealCurves that can testify and show you their bags—the money is real.

At the end of the day, every dancer should be able to rely on the Holy Trinity (Sex Appeal, Hustle, and Game) to obtain their goals. What are you bringing to the table and how can you maximize on your skills? It's easy to go "under the knife" for a possible quick fix, but do you have the courage and the determination to sharpen *your* knife?

Just because you get some "work done"

doesn't mean you have automatically enhanced your Sex Appeal. It also does't mean you upped your Hustle and Game.

Case in point, if you were known as the Professional Air dancer with a flat ass and a snobby attitude and you get some ass shots, it's only a matter of time before patrons will secretly label you the Professional Air Dancer with the same snobby attitude with ass shots. Yes, the game is that simple. You were hoping for a bigger bag, but nothing changed except for the conversation.

If you are considering leaving #TeamNatural, and think the pros outweigh the cons, before you take that step, you must ask yourself the following introspective questions:

Are you getting the "work done" so you can attract more investors or are you secretly trying to impress and slay the dancers in your dressing room? Who are you competing with? What are you competing for?

Because your choice does come with consequences. Creating a compelling visual shouldn't be a life or death decision.

DANCER NOTE

In an environment fueled by the desire to see T and A, it's vital that you invest in your appearance and create an eye-catching experience that is captivating and compelling.

LAW
4

HARNESS YOUR ENERGY

The power of positive energy will always defeat negative vibes.

—Unknown

As you sit quietly in your sanctuary, focused on creating a compelling visual, you are now ready to harness your energy in the right direction—a *positive* direction. Consider this transition to be the stripper version of the law of attraction. It's time to get to the money and this law is about igniting the power of positive energy.

The process of harnessing your energy is not rooted in mysticism. No scented candles or sage incense sticks are needed, and you definitely don't need to roll out a yoga mat and do poses to balance your root chakra (although stretching is recommended). You certainly don't have to decorate the dressing room with air-purifying plants and a few Chinese money trees to cultivate a *feng shui* environment.

The first step is **self-acceptance**.

You must deal with the present.

Do not get caught up thinking about the reasons why you're in the jungle putting on clear platform heels and applying your favorite body spray. Do not feel sorry for yourself or carry a "woe is me" attitude. Simply accept your current situation and embrace your role as an exotic dancer. You made the decision. You're not in Kansas anymore and this is no fairy tale. You're about to hit the stage and "flash for cash."

It is what it is—for now!

Don't turn back, face the music.

Before you leave the dressing room, look confidently into the mirror and take the sacred oath. These affirming words will empower you and be a reminder that you are a lioness who has the strength and the necessary hunting skills to conquer the jungle—it's showtime! And there's money out there with your name on it.

I AM AN EXOTIC DANCER,
THE JUNGLE IS MY DOMAIN.
I OWN THE STAGE,
YOU WILL REMEMBER MY NAME.
I WILL SECURE THAT BAG,
I WILL COLLECT HEAVY RAIN.
THE STRIPPER GODS ARE WITH ME
AS I MASTER THIS GAME.

This oath is transparent. It's straightforward and clear-cut. Recite the oath and let the words grab you and compel you to aggressively seize the moment. You are about to catwalk into the eye of the storm, but guess what? You are mentally and physically up for the challenge. You look good, feel good and smell good—the stripper trifecta!

The bag is all yours—it's outside on the main floor waiting for you. You can taste it. Your positive spirit and vigor naturally propel you to the second step: **visualization**.

In the words of the great American motivational speaker, Zig Ziglar:

If you don't see yourself as a winner, then you cannot perform as a winner.

You must see yourself winning. Visualize yourself on stage, killing your showcase and watching the money come down like New Year's Eve confetti. Visualize the appearance of the magic broom and the heap of cash being swept up by your favorite muscular bouncer. Look forward to sipping on your go-to cocktail as you anticipate the thirsty compliments and welcome the free-spirited conversation. Picture your Regular's eyes lighting up as you deliver a mind-fucking lap dance that makes him empty his checking and savings account. Smirk as you foresee the cheesy grin on your face while you count your bag at the end of the night.

When you're mentally prepared for the challenge and you see yourself winning, essentially, you are harnessing your energy in the right direction. You are on the positive side of things.

You are ready to eat.

For starters, digest this timeless stripper maxim:

YOUR ENERGY INTRODUCES YOU BEFORE YOU TWERK

If you want to eat, you must understand that before you utter a single word, announce your stage name, or do a single pole trick, your energy will speak for you.

Do make sure it's positive.

Energy is powerful and contagious. It radiates throughout the room and acts as your representative. It's the first stage of non-verbal communication. Your aura and sexual swagger make a palpable impression that can break the ice even before you see it.

Unlike a dark cloud of negative energy, positive energy emanates a glow that energizes your sex appeal and taps into your sacred femininity. Naturally, you stand out and attract prosperity, becoming a magnet for excess and adulation. That stripper spirit invigorates your hustle and brings out one of your prized possessions—your smile. Delivering a natural, genuine smile is like striking a patron with a lightning bolt. It can freeze time and paralyze an eager patron who can't wait to spend their hard-earned money. The buck doesn't stop there:

Positive energy can have you catwalking by a patron and your sexy vibes alone will force them to grab a waitress and ask for your stage name. They start calculating their budget, thinking about how many lap dances they can squeeze in and what couch to occupy.

Positive energy will have a thirsty patron running to the DJ booth asking for your whereabouts and waiting patiently for your return from the VIP area. Hours can go by, but that wink of an eye that you delivered is still imprinted in that patron's brain.

Positive energy disarms a reluctant patron who wants to experience a memorable time but feels uneasy and stressful from his workday. Your smile and cool vibes make him feel relaxed and royal as he orders a round of drinks and requests a stack of singles.

Positive energy can make a Sugar Daddy sign up for a therapy session on your favorite couch without knowing all your qualifications and specialties. He's drawn to your stripper spirit and care-free attitude. He wants that energy to rub off on him and he's willing to pay big money for your presence.

Positive energy has a wide-eyed patron running to an ATM and making a big withdrawal, before you can even get a chance to say hello and pick their brain. They can already picture themselves being your captive and under your spell.

Positive energy will have a shy couple

choose you out of hundreds of dancers and feel comfortable telling you their secret fantasies and desires. They can't help but to speak freely and relish the moment under your sexy aura.

And you know who else responds to **positive energy**? The Stripper Gods. They only bestow blessings upon those who work hard and persevere with optimism. They know exactly what you're dealing with and the challenges that you face in the jungle. They're divinely aware of the specific dollar amount that you need to make—for the shift, the week, the month, and so forth. Knowing your financial goals and seeing through your alter-ego and underneath your thick skin is their specialty.

Have you ever noticed that whenever you receive a blessing from the Stripper Gods, you're always exhausted from working multiple shifts and performing for empty compliments? You were ready to call it quits, but you decided to keep twerking and remain optimistic. Then, all of a sudden, a mysterious patron named George comes out of nowhere and showers you with tips as if it was your birthday! Just like that, you made your goal. You almost shed tears of joy as you looked up into the sky and said, "Thank you, Stripper Gods." The lesson?

Every dollar has a silver lining.

With every mercy tip, every trickle of light rain, and each crumpled up dollar bill that you receive from a demeaning game of stripper darts, there is always a brighter day with a green carpet and a hefty bag of money at the end of it. You have to believe wholeheartedly that your bag will be filled and your goals will be met. Always stay positive through the ups and downs, and never allow yourself to feel defeated. Once you fall victim to discouragement and self-doubt, that negative energy will severely affect your hustle. And a *scared* hustle don't make no money. A pessimistic vibe takes over you, causing you to become impatient and overbearing—borderline desperate—actions that curse the Stripper Gods and their merciful power.

The Stripper Gods help those who help themselves.

If there's one thing they dislike, it's a dancer who has a feeling of entitlement; a snobbish vibe that reeks with immaturity. Nothing in the jungle is given. You can't pout and stomp your way into getting that bag. You have to be on the hustle. When you start to think about what you deserve and not what you earn, that attitude will leave you out of favor with the Stripper Gods. And being left alone in the jungle to fend for yourself without divine intervention and mercy is a daunting task, even for the most experienced dancers.

DANCER NOTE

Positive energy is powerful. It not only attracts a positive cash flow but it's contagious and inviting. It gives your sex appeal and personality a natural glow that is irresistible to any patron looking for a fun time.

LAW

5

TRANSFORM INTO YOUR STAGE
NAME

*When I go onstage, I kind of turn into a beast
sometimes, this alter-ego, you know.*

—Nicole Scherzinger

When you're finally dressed to kill, draped in
your favorite outfit, and you've taken the sacred
oath, it's now time to flip the switch. Once you take
your first step onto the main floor, you are no longer
your government name—it doesn't exist.

The jungle is calling you and it's calling you
by another name.

Like a football player leaving the tunnel to

be introduced into the starting lineup, it's game time and this requires you to go into beast mode. But keep in mind, your game is way more intense than anything on a gridiron.

You're an independent contractor and you didn't receive a large signing bonus and a hefty salary to suit up in your stripper uniform. You actually have to pay to play; hence the house fee and tip out that you have to sacrifice. When bills are due, you can't rely on your Regulars to visit you on any given Sunday. The grind is daily and the season is all year long.

Entering this game will demand a *new* you.

And when your stage name is announced by the DJ, similar to a superstar athlete, that's your signal to tighten up your G-string, wipe down the pole, and get to work. You're on the clock, money is on the line, and it's time to eat or be eaten. More importantly, you are now a manifestation of your stage name.

A stage name represents more than just a catchy title that can start a flirty conversation. It represents a transformation that is necessary to function at a high-level in an environment that will try to eat away at your inner truth. Your stage name is protection; it's your first line of defense; a mental wall that creates a healthy separation between the *real* you and your jungle persona.

Can you imagine the DJ welcoming you to the stage using your real name? And then a drunk patron asking you for a lap dance and trying to talk dirty in your ear using your real name? That's beyond cringe-worthy. It's strip club blasphemy! That level of exposure ruins the very game that is being played and destroys the psychological wall that is vital to creating a strip club fantasy.

Why do you think it's so important for the average, unworthy patron to know your real name?

For many, it's a legitimate goal. You may consider it inconsequential or extremely annoying, but they know that the more you're willing to be an open book, the easier it is to chip away at your hidden truths. It's human nature. You're not a robot. Even with a protective barrier, it's still natural to yearn for an open and honest conversation with a selected person and reveal parts of your being, albeit on certain levels. In general, hearing one's real name in a sincere fashion is one of the best compliments in the world. It's a simple gesture that speaks volumes. Sooner or later, the more you hear it, the more you open up.

Their agenda is to get you to expose your wounds and scars, so they can slide in and provide the band-aid and solution. It all starts with your real name. Scaling that wall is the first step to trying to get to know the real you.

This is why choosing a proper stage name is crucial to your existence in the jungle. It's not just something you pull out of a hat. It's a decision that needs to be given serious thought. It's not only a built-in defense mechanism that preserves your sanity and safeguards your personal identity, but it should also trigger your alter-ego. The right stage name awakens your inner savage and releases the hustler inside of you that lays dormant in the outside world.

Strategically, you can certainly have more than one. You can be a stripper ninja and move covertly throughout your local jungles with several different stage names. It's an easy way to duck and dodge your undesirable patrons who can't take the hint that you don't want to "Netflix and chill." But whatever name you choose to go by, make sure your stage name represents a strong connection to that alter ego and symbolizes your brand and what you offer the jungle.

The choice is yours. You can turn into a superwoman or a super freak, or a combination of both.

It can be a subtle yet sexy girl-next-door persona (**Courtney, Nadia, Natasha, Billie, Nina, Alice, April, Katrina, Gianni, Kelly, Vanessa**) or a more blatant, fun-filled attitude (**Fire, Danger, Trouble, Red, Bossy, Feisty, Maverick, Khaleesi**).

Or you can be a traveler and take your Regulars on exotic trips (**Egypt, Brazil, Sahara, Jersey, Miami, Milan, Dallas, Paris, Korea,**

Tokyo, Asia, Russia).

If you're into brand names, you can always flaunt your popular status (**Gucci, Dior, Hennessy, Mercedes, Porsche, Chanel**).

Your name can also highlight a body part (**Dimples, Apple, Apple Bottom, Peaches, Cakes, Mellony**).

And, of course, if you're obsessed with celebrities, you can take your pick (**Marilyn M, Kim K, Madonna, Aaliyah, Sade**).

As you already know, the possibilities are endless.

Bunny, Eve, Angel, Karma, Lust, Mary Jane, Daisy…

The amount of stage names that are used and created on a nightly basis can rival the number of stars in the sky. But the objective is still the same. Select a name that can elicit a transformation inside of you. Only when you've fully transformed and you embody your brand can you execute your agenda and activate your superpowers.

Yes, your **superpowers**. When you're in the zone, fully locked in as [Insert Stage Name Here], and living in the moment, you can get in touch with your three main superpowers:

Stripper Intuition. That's the little voice inside of you that will be assisting as you navigate through the jungle and its cast of characters. Unfortunately, money isn't the only thing around the corner;

snakes, rats, and perverts are waiting for you to stumble and fall. When things get sketchy, that intuitive voice will tell you who to ignore or when to flee a situation that may seem hazardous to your safety.

Your stripper intuition will also tell you when you're putting too much sauce into your alter-ego and overplaying your hand to the point where you're coming off phony and disingenuous—the telltale signs of a scammer. You know what's worse than an actress? A terrible actress that overacts and feigns interest. One who's conversation sounds scripted, and straight out of a cheesy porn movie. To seize the moment is to feel the moment, and it's better to improvise and go with the flow instead of trying to win an Oscar.

X-Rated Vision. This vision allows you to see through patron's pockets and spot the true investors. In the jungle, you will encounter Spectators, Pretenders, Rejectors, Pimps, and many others who will be there to waste your time. And we all know that time is money. Although you wish for every patron to be a Whale with deep pockets, you will learn to appreciate the average patron who simply wants to blow a check (big or small) and have a good time. Dealing with the alternative on the daily is depressing. Too many patrons come to the club to hog space and wear binoculars so they can enjoy the free show from afar. Having the X-rated vision to quickly find an angel investor in a crowd full of tightwads is a superpower that saves time and adds efficiency to your hunting skills.

Force Field. When your energy is high and you're emanating a positive vibe, a force field surrounds you that makes it easier to detect negative vibrations coming from others—especially patrons. This force field naturally helps you to deflect or temporally block their verbal attacks that are aimed to penetrate your psyche and affect your self-esteem. Instead of telling them to "talk to the hand," the field's brightness blinds them with positive energy. Once again, misery loves company and some patrons are hell-bent on dragging you down to their miserable level. Haters and distractors are also looking to knock you off your game and take away your confidence. But never let anyone dim your stripper shine. Your force field along with your stripper intuition are powerful weapons that keep you away from those who want to block your prosperity.

When you can activate all three of your superpowers, you know you've made a successful transformation into your stage name. And every superstripper needs a good stage name.

DANCER NOTE

An ideal stage name should tap into your alter-ego and ultimately protect your everyday persona. It's a torch that leads you through the jungle as you stay focused on your agenda.

LAW
6

ENHANCE THE FANTASY

We don't create a fantasy world to escape reality.
We create it to be able to stay.

—Lynda Barry

This law is about a magic word that represents so much to the strip club industry. It possesses a quality that knows no bounds and no limitations; and for patrons, it has no restraints, judgments or censorship. Most movers and shakers in the business will tell you that it's the #1 selling point. That word is **Fantasy**.

But first off, what is *the* fantasy?

Simple answer:

A man's primary fantasy is access to a variety of
attractive women without the fear of rejection.

— Warren Farrell

Bullseye! That's the strip club environment in a nutshell—a wide variety of exotic dancers dwelling in one location. Add in a nice touch of carnality (fleshy and sensual lap dances) and some timely goosebumps and the fantasy seems so real that patrons can devour it with all five senses (sight, hearing, smell, touch, and the fantasy of taste). If the patron has enough money to play the game and play it right, they can live out the ultimate orgiastic fantasy; the only thing rejected is their sexual advances.

Once you consider all the masks, the nuances of behavior, and the different agendas of the modern-day strip club goer, you can strip away the facade and narrow things down to the following strip club fantasies:

69
SEX
A DATE
ORAL SEX
A SEXCAPADE
A SEXUAL ORGY
A "MOVIE" NIGHT
A ONE-NIGHT STAND
A PRIVATE RENDEZVOUS
A CHANCE TO CATCH A
TIGER BY ITS TAIL
AND
A MÉNAGE À TROIS

Oh, you forget it was a hedonistic entrapment; a jungle full of lustful animals? With the ACE up your sleeve, you confidently catwalk the main floor, discreetly looking for a target. You spot a patron at an open table. Immediately, your stripper intuition tells you that he's a good prospect for Team [**Insert Stage Name Here**].

After seductively locking eyes, he motions for you to come join him. You sashay over, gliding like a tiger and take a seat.

Pleasantries are exchanged. Drinks are ordered. The game begins. Or shall we say, your game heats up. You see a potential Regular. It's time to enhance the fantasy. Now, this goes beyond the typical, formulaic introduction:

What's your name?
Is this your first time here?
Where are you from?
What do you do?
Would you like a lap dance?

In the beginning, you can stick to the script by reciting strip club gospel (Sapphire 3:16) and go with the flow. Naturally, some patrons will end up being a quick kill. You have a brief chitchat and then head to a booth, perform a mouthwatering lap dance and send them on their way—on to the next. You proceed to devour more simpletons, chew 'em and spit out the bones.

Every single patron can't fall under the title of Regular. To have 1,000 Regulars is to have no Regulars.

So, when you scan the room with your X-rated vision and you identify a long-term investor, that's when you turn it up a notch and mix in some truth with a few little lies and occasional vulnerability. They say men fall in love (mainly lust) with their eyes, but don't think for one second that men don't have a strong ear for words, especially those that can tap into their lustful imagination— and therein lies the keys to your seductiveness.

What the eyes see and the ears hear, the mind believes.

—Harry Houdini

To truly enhance the fantasy is to prolong the fantasy by initiating a never-ending game of cat and mouse. Where the patron believes that they're the cool cat on the chase, but in actuality, you're the ferocious feline orchestrating the game—using your yarn string as puppet strings, playfully making the mouse forfeit their cheese and fall into your trap.

Your goal is to not only secure the bag, but to acquire a client base of Regulars that invest in your brand on a consistent and continual basis, so in return, you can secure more bags—that's career sustainability.

In the jungle, stability is hard to come by and it's only achieved through Regulars and the ability to keep your stripper money cycle in constant rotation—it takes work. Not everyone can reel in a Sugar Daddy.

This is where your body language, use of words, and your persona play an integral part in your seduction. The power of touch goes without question. Even the most unskillful dancer can point to the drool coming from a patron's mouth after giving a high-mileage lap dance as Exhibit A. But it's the eyes and the ears that you have to capture, to weave your magical spell.

THE FIVE KEY PRINCIPLES TO ENHANCING THE FANTASY

Apply these five key principles to your repertoire and mix them into your stratagem, creating a witches' brew of exotic (Enticing, X-Rated, Open-minded, Teasing, Intoxicating, Captivating) ingredients that mesmerize a patron's five senses and make them come back for more.

PRINCIPLE 1: PERFECT THE LOOK

Every seducer knows the power of eye contact. Eyes are the window to the soul. And if you can perfect that "stripper look"—a look that can freeze a patron from across the room and instantly speak the language of the jungle; a look that can see through a patron's mask and mentally undress them with your eyes—you can always put them in a trance. Your eyes can say it all.

The right amount of eye contact with the right level of intensity has a mesmerizing effect that stirs engagement. Give a patron a passionate glare while on stage, a fiery glance back during a sexy lap dance, or just a spirited gaze as you enjoy your cocktail and listen to them tell you stories about life, you can make a patron feel *special, valued* and *appreciated*. Regardless of how cheesy and fluffy that may sound. It's the truth. That look leaves a lasting impression on a patron's psyche.

In an animalistic environment, some things aren't that complicated.

But keep in mind that this look doesn't need to be overdramatized. When you're in the zone, vibing off your own sex appeal and stripper spirit, the look should be genuine. You see something you like. Whether it's a bank account, a patron's smile, or a ripe opportunity, the more genuine the look, the more you can enhance the fantasy and maintain a connection.

REALITY

You have to realize that in a world addicted to smartphones, people are becoming more anti-social with many lacking true intimacy and the feeling of simple acknowledgement, let alone being thirsted for in a lustful way. Most people don't share eye contact, and if so, it's only for a couple of nanoseconds and then people go back to their cocoons with their head down and headphones on. But inside a strip club, you have the opportunity to provide that missing connection that all people desire—a like-minded person who's willing to look into your soul and confirm your existence. You possess that power.

PRINCIPLE 2: TELL BEAUTIFUL LIES

Telling beautiful lies are not only necessary for protecting your personal identity and safety, but they enhance the fantasy by creating a playful dialogue full of flattery, roleplay, and enticement; allowing you to be elusive and cunning like a cat. And patrons love the challenge of trying to corner the frisky cat. You've heard 'em all:

"Are you single?"
"What's your *real* name?"
"Where do you live?"
"Can I take you out?"
"What are you doing later tonight?"
"Do you find me attractive?"

The list of questions is long, but the beautiful thing about the jungle is you have the permission to become a ballerina and dance around the truth. You can avoid answering certain questions with style and grace—tiptoeing and bending around them. The truth is powerful and, similar to trust, it has to be earned over time. There's nothing wrong with making a patron go through hoops to obtain your hidden truths.

Truth consists not in never lying but in knowing when to lie and when not to do so.

—Samuel Butler

Telling a patron what you want them to know and having them follow your narrative is essential when playing a game of cat and mouse. It's very simple, if you're sitting with a patron that you think is ugly—one that you can't find remotely attractive at all—then nothing will spark an interest other than the faces of the dollar bills you receive. You don't have to go overboard and tell that patron that you think he's the sexiest man alive—that's just a lie. But there's also no strategic advantage in being brutally honest and telling him that you think he's ugly and that you'd rather him cover up his face and just hand over the cash. You have to know when to elegantly dance around the truth and tell a beautiful lie that keeps the fantasy vivid and appeasing. Whether you know it or not, you're a storyteller—a strip club oracle of sorts and you have to be a mistress when it comes to words and the language of the jungle.

However, you should never find yourself having to tell the most heart-wrenching lies to play the game and scavenge money. Tales of how your car broke down and your landlord is about to kick you out, and if you don't come up with $1,000, you'll be homeless. That's not seductive, beautiful nor bewitching. You're just coming off as a liar and a fantasy killer.

REALITY

As highlighted in Law 5 of *The 21 Laws of Surviving a Gentlemen's Club*—Read Between The Lies, this quote by the great poet and philosopher, Ralph Waldo Emerson, eloquently details a dirty secret about life: "Truth is beautiful, without doubt; but so are lies."

The reality is that people prefer to hear a lie. Most people don't want to hear the truth—they run from it. They sprinkle sugar on it. They put it in a box, wrap it and attach a nice bow on top. Rarely is a person honest and upfront with their thoughts and intentions. The truth hurts, and because it's so raw, it's hard to swallow. And on top of that, it's boring and bland. It forces one to be accountable and who wants to be accountable when you can live a beautiful lie—a fantasy? Lies are entertaining, especially those that tickle your fancy and boost the ego. So, inside the jungle, patrons welcome the beautiful lies as long as they match their level of escapism. No one makes return visits to hear the truth, they want the fantasy.

PRINCIPLE 3: THE ART OF FINESSE

When it comes to your words and body

language, avoid overacting and over-exaggerating your interest. Leave that for the patron's imagination. No one likes to long-term invest in a bad actress who spouts out scripted dialogue as if starring in a low-budget B movie. Every time you give a compliment, the phoniness is written all over your face. Without a doubt, putting too much sauce in your witches' brew will ruin its potency.

Less is always more.

There's never a need to overplay your hand in a game that you control. You must **Finesse** the situation. You don't finesse with a hard sell and a cheesy ultimatum; that's when you're "doing too much." The art of finesse is to come off as genuine as possible; smooth and seductive, flirty and persuasive in your persona.

When you transform into your stage name and become your alter-ego—not your fake-ego—it should be a natural transition, almost second nature. Because your alter-ego is a real part of your being, it shouldn't be phony or fake. When you tell beautiful lies, they are not some grandiose story filled with over the top drama or corny lines that a patron can see through with ease. No acting awards will be given out during your shift.

The art of finesse is the art of realism.

You are just being you—sexy, cool and fun.

And when you tell a patron, "It's good to see you. How have you been?" Those simple words go a long way to making the fantasy seem so real. The more natural you appear, the more powerful your allure. You'll always seem attainable and never out of reach. You are now finessing the situation.

REALITY

The reality is, everyone knows that it's a game. The jungle is a stage and everyone is playing their part, contributing to the overall strip club experience—even down to the restroom attendant. There are more than enough masks, scripted lines and personas to go around in this theatrical play called "Enhance the Fantasy." So, it is pointless to try to become the most dramatic actress of all-time and blatantly remind patrons at every step that they are in a fantasyland and everything is for show. You must play the game and play it well. You can't orchestrate an entrancing game of cat and mouse if you want to make a mockery of the game and "meow" every second. There is no longevity in pushing that reality.

PRINCIPLE 4: FIND THE BUTTON

Every patron has one. Unlike a panic button, this is a button that's begging to be pushed. It can instantly stimulate a patron's mind and mentally send them into a fantasyland—another dimension—the Stripper Zone. A place where they feel free to express their wildest thoughts. The button is usually a deep, dark, sexual fantasy or a strange curiosity about a topic that they wouldn't dare to discuss with the average person. It could also be the sound of a voice, a penchant for dirty talk, or a secret foot fetish. It could be the smell of a sweet scent or just the mere sight of fishnets gripping a juicy body. Whatever it is, if you can find that button and tap it, you will create an intimate bond between you and the patron. You will have the power and influence to spark that patron's imagination and enhance the fantasy through closeness and secrecy. They will gravitate to you as a welcoming escape from reality and judgment. Why not? You are fun, carefree and, most of all, open-minded. You embody the escapism that patrons seek on every visit.

REALITY

Every mature adult has secrets, quirks, and fantasies that they keep to themselves. Not even their closest friends or significant other are aware of these hidden treasures. Some may be quite laughable or embarrassing and others may border on perversion, depending on who you talk to. But those items normally stay confidential and safely guarded. However, there is always an urge to share those items with someone that brings a level of comfort and openness; a relatable person that can listen without giving harsh judgment and consequence. And the reality is, the strip club is one of the few environments where hidden truths and racy conversations make their way to the surface, but yet, they remain in the dark. You are indeed part of a secret society.

PRINCIPLE 5: OPEN THE BOOK

Make the patron an open book that you can scroll through the pages with ease, flipping back and forth, reviewing and jumping through chapters, highlighting key paragraphs for further reference. Using money as a bookmark, you want to learn the patron's life story and use that privy information to develop a psychological relationship with their mind. But instead of a licensed psychologist, you are the sexy librarian who puts on a pair of reading glasses and reads between the lines and analyzes their story with inquisitiveness. You are asking the right questions, curiously picking their brain like you would an author who's written a classic novel about ambition, desire, and untamed lust. In return, they are engaged, loyal and totally interested in giving you the inside scoop. They appreciate their #1 reader.

On the other hand, you are rarely an open book. Most patrons get your carefully written cliff notes that provide just enough intrigue for them to pry for more personal information. You can already anticipate the inquiries:

"So, when are you gonna tell me your *real* name?"
"How are things going with you and your boyfriend?"
"Is he okay with you dancing?"
"Let me take you on a trip?"

As should be, they want to get to the meat of your black book. And if they want a more revealing conversation—and they always do—they have to stay longer to read more from your official manuscript. But only the chapters that you want to expose. That's game!

Now, if you prefer to be an open book—a straight shooter—right from the onset, you must be a series of books with multiple storylines, surprise plots and twists. This is the way to keep the fantasy and intrigue going. Who really likes a simple story that is predictable and familiar to the ear? There is no such thing as a boring cat and mouse story. Every visit to the jungle brings a brand-new adventure.

REALITY

Everyone has a story and most people yearn for the chance to reveal their story to a person they deem trustworthy and on the same level. Or sometimes they just like to hear the sound of their own voice. It's human nature. We all want to be acknowledged and to have someone validate our existence by giving an open ear, making us feel alive and interesting. Even in a strip club, where patrons wear a mask, behind that mask is a person that desires to be an open book for that one special exotic dancer who can become a key character in their life story—preferably the chapters that deal with fantasy and eroticism.

DANCER NOTE

The power of touch is undeniable, but to truly enhance the fantasy, you must capture the eyes and ears of the patron. That is where the imagination resides and the fantasy begins—and hopefully for you, the fantasy never ends.

LAW
7

EVERY DOLLAR COUNTS

*One and one is two, and two and two is four, and
five will get you ten if you know how to work it.*

—Mae West

This law is about having the right mentality
to survive the ups and downs of the ever-changing
money flow and avoid stripper stagnation. It's no
secret that it's all about the money. Whatever name
you choose to use: Cash, Moolah, Paper, Bread,
Chips, Racks, Bandz, Bricks, Cheese, Gouda, etc. If
you want to be futuristic, you can throw in
cryptocurrencies like Bitcoin. But the short-term
goal is still the same. Devour your prey, secure the

bag and finish the night off by turning into a money counting machine.

And although you'd prefer for every dollar bill to have Benjamin Franklin's arrogant smirk, the beautiful part about money is that it all adds up, ever-so-easily.

However, outsiders and distractors will try to dim your shine. They love to point out the measly $1 bills on the messy floor that are swiftly picked up while dollar diving, but only you know the true power of the first president, George Washington. He multiplies like no other. And if his other constituents join the party (Abraham Lincoln, Alexander Hamilton, Andrew Jackson, Ulysses S. Grant, and the anti-social Thomas Jefferson), you can gladly say it was a profitable day at the office.

But just like any job, there are good days and bad days—or better yet, good days and *slow* days.

In the jungle, you can have a "movie" type of night where you see nothing less than $20 bills and then the next day, you're dodging crumpled up singles being thrown at you for amusement. Some days, you're staring at your phone, waiting for your shift to end, nervous that you might not have enough money for tip out. Other days, there will be so much rain that you should've worn a raincoat and used an umbrella as a prop in your stage performance. And then the showers disappear and the rest of the week is so dead, that you find yourself in the dressing room, looking into the mirror and questioning why you decided to become an exotic dancer in the first place.

The ups and downs of the ever-changing money flow are no joke, and those slow days will surely come. It's a part of the game. Even your most trusted Regulars miss appointments and can switch up on you, leaving you empty-handed.

Given that you have to seize the moment and utilize your time efficiently, it's easy to apply too much pressure on yourself and become preoccupied with how much money you're making every second, every minute, every hour, and every shift. It's understandable. You don't want your stripper money cycle to stagnate and lose momentum.

But never let yourself become shorted-sighted and bogged down by the unrealistic expectations of an environment that is inherently unpredictable—missing the broader picture. You have to constantly adapt and stay the course. With the right frame of mind, you should appreciate every dollar and focus on the simple fact that they go a long way to helping you achieve your endgame.

1 + 1 = 2

When it comes to receiving tips, the more the merrier, but never belittle or look down on a small tip given by a rookie or the truck driver sitting in the corner. Getting caught up in what you think is "below expectation" is impractical.

The size of the tip is not always a reflection of your stature in the jungle. There are so many variables at play, so it is important to keep things in perspective.

Whether a patron is making it drizzle, providing a rainstorm or holding on to that one dollar bill like their life depended on it, always think about your agenda. A $1 tip here, a $3 tip there, a $60 lap dance over there, and some rain from the stage, turns $425 into $500—Boom! You hit your target without getting in your own way. You kept your eyes on the prize and it feels good.

This is why count up is such a joyful event—it's almost orgasmic—all your twerking, grinding, pole tricks, beautiful lies, and tolerance has led you to the basic principles of addition. It's that energy and attitude that will come in handy when you face the deadliest word in the jungle—**DROUGHT**.

A drought is not to be mistaken for the normal day-to-day fluctuations of the money flow.

It's common knowledge that **Day-Shifts** *are less crowded with patrons and the opportunities for heavy rain are very limited. But if you can lure in a big fish or a loyal investor who enjoys a more intimate atmosphere with fewer Spectators, the Day-Shift is a secret location in the jungle, where you can have one-on-one fun—think quality over quantity.* **Night-Shifts** *are the ideal time for hunting, patrons are in larger groups wandering around in the dark, waiting to be* *ambushed. Although you have to sort through the Spectators, Pretenders, and Rejectors, you have more opportunities to strike and find a patron with juicy pockets.*

But a drought is far from your typical slow day that can be encountered during a Day-Shift or a Night-Shift. A drought is caused by climate change: internal and external forces. Some are a direct result from a rigid management decision or business issues in the concrete jungle that spill and indirectly affect the club's business and bottom line.

You always have to keep an eye out for climate change in the jungle.

CAUSES OF DROUGHT

- Temporary loss of liquor license.
- A rival club opens up and top dancers jump ship, leaving the club and talent level in shambles.
- Management implement new lap dance rules that Regulars and investors silently protest.
- Management targets and caters to a new, trendier customer base, indirectly sending away locals and Regulars.
- Too many nosy bouncers interrupting private lap dances and interrogating patrons, sending them to a more relaxed environment with less chaperoning.

- The relocation of a sports franchise takes away a significant amount of traffic during a particular season.
- The private party sector has become more profitable for dancers, leaving the club with less talent.
- Local law enforcement and the rumors of undercover cops have runway business.
- Hit-and-miss Holiday season. When a miss, patrons save their money.

Recessions can also hit the jungle, so stay alert. Hopefully, you appreciated every dollar because when shit hits the fan, you don't want to be digging through your couch for loose change.

CAUSES OF RECESSIONS

- The club closes its doors; terminates its lease and relinquishes its alcohol permit.
- Alcohol and Tobacco Commission (ATC) and Vice raid the club for various violations, shutting down the business indefinitely.
- City ordered shut-down.
- Men go on a strip club strike.
- An actual Great Depression hits the U.S.

A drought (or a recession) leads to another word that is detrimental to your stripper money cycle. That word is desperation; where you're the one salivating and thirsty for every single dollar. Not a good look! Once you're desperate, that's when the wolves come out. They can smell the fact that you haven't been counting every dollar and now they believe you're at the mercy of the dollar bill. Disrespect ensues.

Stay strong and mentally ready so you don't have to get ready. That attitude is what you need to survive the ups and downs, the droughts and anything else that will stagnate your money flow.

DANCER NOTE

Always stay focused on the big picture. No matter whose face is on the dollar bill, every dollar counts toward your short-term and long-term goals. Before you can secure the bag, you must first appreciate what constitutes a bag.

LAW
8

EMBRACE REJECTION

*Rejection just motivates me to keep trying and to try
to do better.*

—Sasha Grey

This law is about a part of the game that is
plainly unavoidable. For some, it can be the thorn in
their side, and for others, it can awaken their inner
stripper spirit, motivating them to secure that bag at
all costs.

If you're a true hustler—proactive and dead
serious about your agenda, then you're all too
familiar with rejection.

Some try their best to avoid it. There are

"stage dancers" who prefer to only dance on stage and avoid the savagery and the carnage happening between the dancers and the patrons on the main floor; the flirty conversations and the mental and physical chess matches. They'd rather twerk in their safe space and settle for drizzles of light rain, hoping for heavier showers to come. Whether purposely choosing to work at an exotic club that heavily promotes the "making it rain" culture or simply wanting to shy away from one-on-one contact, consequently, they are cutting off a major source of revenue: the lap dance.

But an exotic dancer does not live by tips alone.

That's why you should venture off outside of the stage; stay active and assertive in your pursuit to make your designated dollar mount, and thrive by this old school quote:

A closed mouth don't get fed.

As you stay true to this bit of wisdom through your open attempts at seduction and your play with words, the conversation should lead up to you asking this pivotal question, "Would you like a lap dance?"

Before you receive an answer, you should already be used to this fact: you will get turned down.

No matter how fine you are, how amazing

your body, or how sweet your personality—it will happen. And it will happen often. You must embrace it. It's happened to the best in the business. It happens to the dancer that you secretly have a stripper crush on, that you think is flawless.

No dancer is immune to rejection.

It can come from:

THE NERD
THE LOCAL
THE COUPLE
THE CIVILIAN
THE LESBIAN
THE ROOKIE
THE SIMPLETON
THE PARTY ANIMAL
THE MARRIED MAN
THE DRUG DEALER
THE AVERAGE JOE
THE GENTLEMAN
THE GANGSTER
AND EVEN FROM
THE REGULAR.

It comes with the territory.

There are so many different stage names and flavors to choose from that you'll never be everybody's cup of tea. It's essential to keep things in perspective. You're always going be subject to a patron's natural selection. And you can't please every customer. Truth be told, why would you?

The objective is to never let rejection get into your head and affect your psyche. First off, you never take it personally. It's not an attack on your self-worth as an exotic dancer. It's okay to take notes and learn from your experiences, but do not get caught up in the specific reasons for why your services were denied (for the time being). Avoid that rabbit hole at all costs. It only leads to self-doubt, low-confidence, and self-sabotage.

You have to brush it off and stay focused on the big picture.

With the right attitude and game plan, you will understand that there is no such thing as rejection. There's only a "matter of time." Someone *will* take the bait and fall into your trap.

You know it—it's going down.

Embrace the challenge, embrace rejection.

Upon your first interaction with an unfamiliar face, and as you continue to be on the hunt for brand new prey, you will encounter five main types of prospective patrons. Not everyone who walks through the door is a Regular. More importantly, your Regular. That yin and yang relationship takes time to develop. Although you hope for the room to be filled with Sugar Daddies and Whales, the jungle is often full of casual-walk ins, fly-by-nights, and civilians—patrons with no agenda—which is exactly why you never take rejection personally.

You'll find, to your astonishment, that many

come to the strip club to hang out with no intentions of investing in anyone's brand. The reality is, the more establishments try to reinvent the wheel and advertise to a mass-market of patrons, the more you'll have to deal with a mass invasion of onlookers who enter the jungle with a set of binoculars but no bandz.

With experience, you can read a patron's body language (eye contact, posture, arms, hands, personal space), observe their disposition and determine their agenda without wasting valuable time getting flustered and having your G-string in a bunch. Rejection will seem like a minor misstep that can be corrected. Like a hawk, use keen eyesight and patience—scan the room, observe your prey and then strike quickly.

The Observer. This patron likes to chill and observe the scene before indulging. He doesn't like to rush things, and normally, it takes a drink or two for him to warm up. He definitely came to have fun and has plans on disappearing into a VIP booth, but he's not eager to spend his money hastily. This is not his first strip club rendezvous. He's the gentleman that is referred to in the title "Gentlemen's Club."

He works hard for his money, so his time is precious, and he is using it wisely. As a result, he's the type to reject you at first, and even at a second go-round. It can be annoying or even frustrating because you know he came to have a great time. So, what's the wait? You move on to the next, figuring there's no interest.

But later that night, don't be surprised when he's running to the DJ booth desperately asking for your whereabouts and hoping you didn't finish your shift.

The Pretender. If you dance at an exotic club/ urban club, or at a club that pushes the nightclub vibe, more often than not, there will be a lot of pretenders in the room. But they're not always easy to detect. Pretenders look like investors. They are energetic, attentive and always engaged. They love to ask questions while bobbing their head to the beat, dancing with themselves and smiling from ear to ear. They might even get a couple of singles to flash around, to let the dancer know that rain is coming—so they can play the part.

The bold ones take it a step further and sit at a table, holding bricks of cash so they can run their bait and switch technique. But the reality is, they want nothing to do you with you. They are simply there for the party atmosphere. They pretend to be investors, but they never allocated anything in their budget for you and your brand. Pretenders can talk a good game, but they're not about that real " strip club life".

Don't forget that for every "movie" night that takes place in a strip club, where the sky has turned green from all the money in the air and the green carpet treatment is in full effect, there will always be extras on the set.

The Rejector. This patron gets off on rejecting every single dancer that approaches him for a lap dance. It gets to the point that you get hesitant to even come over to his area. Which should never happen if you're a lioness ready to conquer the jungle. But this patron presents a cat-and-mouse challenge that makes you rethink your strategy.

Normally, he'll set up shop at a table with a cocktail and leave a chair open for confident dancers—that's his trap. Once you take a seat, the conversation will start with the typical script. And then you drop the question.

"Would you like a lap dance?"
"Not right now....maybe later."

So, you embrace that rejection and keep it moving. And throughout your shift, and out of the corner of your eye, you notice him turning every single dancer down—even the baddest in the room. You don't get it? Is this the pickiest patron of all-time?

What makes the Rejector unique is what also highlights the uniqueness of the strip club experience. In his everyday life, this patron has always had to pursue women. He's had to chase them, always being the one to initiate contact and to start a conversation. Most women don't know what that truly feels like—to be the one subject to rejection. So, when he enters a strip club and has all sorts of sexy, flavorful, exotic dancers approaching him and courting his money, this is a welcoming break from the norm. To him, rejecting offers is the worth the price of admission.

The Selector. This patron may come off like a Rejector or an Observer but if you examine closely and look at the determination in his eyes, your stripper intuition will give you a hunch. You'll notice that he's relaxed, but also extremely focused and locked in, as if on a mission or a scheduled appointment. Every other second, he's discretely scanning the room in anticipation of something special. You decide to take a seat and right before you politely introduce yourself—it hits you! It's written all over his face.

Awww. He's waiting for his Favorite!!!

His mind, body, and soul have already made a selection. And he's arrived 15 minutes ahead of schedule. At that point, you try to salvage the brief chitchat and keep it cool, knowing that you have to respect the game. Quite honestly, it was like pulling teeth from a shark. His attention and focus was elsewhere. You feel like he should've just told you he was already spoken for—but you get it. He is doing exactly what you would want your Regular to do. He's saving all his time and resources for his Favorite. This should make you smile and chuckle to yourself as you embrace that type of rejection.

The Spectator. This is the patron that enters the club with no other agenda than to watch the show. The Spectator will find an open table, order a single drink, and pull out a nice set of binoculars. You can approach and flirt all you want, but when you ask the central question, "'Would you like a lap dance?'" He passively rejects your offer. Because of his limited budget, he's certainly not going to entertain the thoughts of a lap dance or a VIP. The DJ can announce a 2 for 1 special, or even better, a 3 for 1 special, and that still won't make him put down his binoculars.

Unlike the Pretender, he doesn't play the part. He doesn't act like he's going to spend any money. He's quite content being the helpless spectator admiring the beauty on stage and the shenanigans on the main floor. Over time, you'll understand and appreciate the Spectator and their voyeuristic ways.

But the main problem happens with when the Spectator tries to get bold and take a seat at the tip rail. Those seats are reserved for serious investors —no binoculars allowed.

OBSERVATION. What makes your job tricky and

difficult to assess is that, in the jungle, there is always a gray area. Things are rarely black and white, and night and day—unlike your work shifts. The environment is unpredictable, full of stories with twists and turns, and characters that constantly change their storylines:

A patron can visit the jungle on a Monday, be flat broke and babysit the same drink for hours, earning him the label of a blue light shopper. A few dancers in the dressing room are clowning him for tipping his meager $3 and for hogging up valuable space that could've been occupied by a big spender. That same patron, can return on a Wednesday and blow a huge check while being held hostage in VIP by you and your sexy partner. He's gladly buying rounds of your favorite cocktails and tipping like a true gentleman. He purposely avoids the dancers that rolled their eyes at him on his previous visit.

What changed?

It's a mix of things. For one: perception. Second: timing, and third: opportunity. His intentions were always in the right place, he just needed his bank account to get on the same page. And that's how the story goes in the jungle.

That's why you have to stay fluid and focused, and don't let rejection stop you from getting that bag.

DANCER NOTE

Rejection is a part of the game. The quicker you can embrace it, the quicker you can use it as motivation and as a way to learn more about your target and their telltale characteristics.

LAW

9

FIND YOUR NICHE

*You gotta keep trying to find your niche and trying
to fit into whatever slot that's left for you or to make
one of your own.*

—Dolly Parton

In the competitive world of exotic dancing,
you have to find a way to stand out from the pack.
It's simply not enough to give yourself a catchy
stage name like Unique or Foreign that signifies
your unrivaled skills and individuality; it sounds
good, but that alone won't do the trick. Having a
distinctive tattoo in the right spot is a good start, but
that ink only scratches the surface. Even throwing
on a slingshot bikini that's thinner than a strand of

dental floss will draw some thirsty looks, but it doesn't guarantee you the spotlight. You will need to do more than setting thirst traps to distinguish yourself in a profession that's oversaturated with sexy and ambitious dancers from all four corners of the earth—different flavors and styles. There's no shortage of links in the stripper food chain.

There's a stripper born every minute.

As long as there are job fairs with blank applications and burgeoning clubs looking to capitalize on the mainstreaming of strip club culture, this influx of newbies and returning veterans will continue around-the-clock. You must find your niche as you navigate the jungle and compete for dollar bills that are floating in the air.

STAGE 1: WHAT ARE YOU WORKIN' WIT'?

It is important to be honest with yourself and quickly figure out your strengths and perceived weaknesses (things you'd like to improve on). What exactly do you bring to the table? What is your specialty? Push your ego to the side, strip away your insecurities and do a mental and physical assessment. With money on the line, you can't afford to be delusional. You must *know thy stripper self.*

Are you a people person? Do you have a quick temper? Do you believe that the tip jar is half full or half empty?

What about your body? Are you a proud member of the #SmallButtsMatter movement? Or are you a card-carrying member of #RealBootiesMatter? Or are you thinking about getting another touch up from your favorite doctor that practices in the rich part of town?

Do you represent the movement of plus-size strippers that have a lot to offer?

You have to be truthful and rational about your skill set.

Rival dancers will be watching you closely, admiring your strong points and playing off your insecurities. It's only smart to be ahead of the game. You of all people need to know yourself more than anyone else. Before you can *show* someone what you're workin' wit, you must *know* what you're workin' wit'.

The Twerker. Can you twerk? No, really, are you a specialist? Can you booty-shake for hours and still keep a patron salivating with their eyes glued to your backside? Can you grab a patron's attention from across the room by making it clap? When you do the scissor leg twerk, can you give a patron a case of strip club vertigo? When you throw your ass in a circle, can you see patrons trying to measure the circumference? When you make your right butt cheek twerk, does it look like you're having a muscle spasm? Are you aware that it's not the size of the booty, but how you work it? Finally, can you travel to Atlanta and hold your own or would you stick out like a sore thumb? If so, then you have a skill that is always in demand and one that allows you to stand out instantly.

The Pole Assassin. Can you attach sparklers to your platforms and perform pole tricks that would have a Romanian gymnast throwing a stack of singles? Can you walk the ceiling like Spiderman and slide back down the pole without making a sound? When you wipe down the pole, does everyone stop and stare knowing you're about to steal the show and garner all the applause? Do dancers constantly ask you questions about your pole routine and comment on your physique? If you opened up a pole dancing class, would your competition bite the bullet and sign up? Can you air walk in the sky and make the Stripper Gods proud? Could you compete in a Pole-A-Thon contest and run away with the bag? If so, then you are a pole assassin who possesses the unique skill to get a standing ovation in a room full of busyness. For a rare moment, you can see a patron bypass their horniness and fully appreciate the *art* of pole dancing.

The Personality. In all seriousness, do you have a great personality? Do you like to talk, chitchat and unknowingly perform the art of seduction? Are you an extrovert who likes to meet strangers and pick their brains and find out what makes them tick— sexually and intellectually? Are you a good listener? Are you able to discuss a wide variety of light-hearted topics and ultimately still direct the conversation towards your goal of securing a bag? Can you be genuine, open-minded, and tell beautiful lies with a warm smile? Do you truly understand that flirtation and playful words can weaken a patron's defenses and open them up like a Christmas gift? Do you also understand that you can achieve your goals without being argumentative and demeaning? If so, the jungle is your smorgasbord.

The Body. Whether natural or surgically enhanced, do you have a body that makes other dancers instantly jealous? When you walk by a patron, does their neck do a 360? Does a wide-eyed patron look you up and down and tell you not to move, and then run to the ATM? Does a young patron have a hard time looking you in the face while you talk because they're too busy admiring the curves on your body? Can you turn a female patron into a savage who wants to do nothing but fondle you and touch you inappropriately? When you walk onto the stage, can you tell that every single patron sitting at the tip rail is thinking about one thing: sex? If so, you'll never have a hard time finding prey.

The Beauty. Do you have a face that is striking? Can you deliver a smile that makes patrons think to themselves, "She's way too pretty to be a stripper?" Can you intimidate a patron and make them freeze up just by giving them a simple glare and a twinkle of an eye? After saying your stage name, do Sugar Daddies submit their applications hoping to become your #1 sponsor? Do you find simpletons staring at you awkwardly and being reluctant to engage? Along with tips, do you always receive business cards from agents and producers looking for the next video vixen, model or porn star? Do ballers and celebrities request your presence at their table so you can give them the look of being the Man? If you possess that type of beauty, take advantage of your time in the jungle.

If you can legitimately combine more than one quality and utilize those qualities to their maximum, the quicker you can enhance the fantasy and create a loyal client base. Keep in mind, this is not about chasing perfection or some imaginary ideal. That is a losing game. This is about versatility, and packaging your skills around a core strength; a distinctive signature. Ideally, you want to be a "**Jane of all trades**." One who has many strengths and various ways to seduce and capture any type of patron. Knowing how to exert your power and intertwine your skills is the sign of a true hustler who knows what they're workin' wit'.

STAGE 2: WHAT IS YOUR PERSONA?

Once you transform into your stage name and tap into your alter-ego, your stripper persona will take over. Why? The jungle is the perfect atmosphere to let your hair down and play by a new set of rules. Inside, you have the freedom to put on a mask and take your everyday persona to a more freaky, uninhibited level. You're not held hostage by the policies and procedures that a HR manager would enforce in corporate America. Hit the main floor, and you can go 0 to 100 with no apologies. It's like taking a daily trip to Las Vegas where you can turn it up a notch and reveal a part of your personality that loves the party scene. But in this case, what happens in the jungle stays in the jungle.

So, what is your persona? Are you even aware you have one? The sooner you realize and identify your persona, the quicker you can take advantage of those characteristics and build a plan of attack based on your style.

Self-awareness is a key to self-mastery.

—Gretchen Rubin

If you want to master this game, self-awareness is everything. A Tiger can't act and emulate the moves of a Hawk. A Hawk can't act and emulate the moves of a Tiger.

The Seducer. You're the mistress of non-verbal communication. Your every sensual movement conveys a singular message: "Meet me in VIP." You like to use slight touch and intense eye contact as ways to draw patrons into your lair. Outside of whispering your stage name, you keep your words to a minimum—short and sweet is your motto. And you always stick to your script by never revealing too much about yourself. You'd rather keep things a mystery than exposing some of your cards. Speaking of games, you like to play a game of cat and mouse, and, of course—you are the ferocious feline.

The Celebrity. When you step onto the main floor, you feel like all eyes are on you—literally all eyes. The jungle is your stage and, according to you, it only comes alive when you arrive. You flip the switch and turn into a Stripper Diva. The spotlight follows you wherever you go. Everything revolves around you. That's how you feel and carry yourself. You do your own thing. You don't even engage with patrons, they have to chase you down or wait patiently for you to speed walk by as they try their best attempt to grab your attention. You already know that money talks, but you prefer it to talk through a megaphone.

The Therapist. Not only do you like conversing with patrons, but you take a particular interest in getting into their heads, listening to their problems and offering advice. You're more than a girl next door who enjoys an easygoing chitchat, you're an uncredited therapist who revels in treating patrons like clients who need pampering and a much-needed ego boost. You provide scheduled therapy sessions, preferably in your office (VIP room). Encouraging patrons to open up and reveal their hidden truths brings a warm smile to your face. You understand that patrons have feelings, and behind their mask and underneath their bravado is a lust for female communication and connection.

The Party Animal. You're the savage. Patrons can see you from a mile away. You can't wait to get a cocktail and hear your favorite strip club anthem. You're aggressive, assertive and anxious to have a great a time. The strip club represents a break from your ordinary life, so when you clock in for work, you're ready to party. Tranquility and patrons who play the background are major turn-offs. They can see it on your face, you clearly don't have time for inactivity. In fact, a dead club is downright depressing and severely irritating to your psyche. That's when you get on the hunt for tequila shots, an open VIP table, and patrons eager to have a party.

The Girl-Next Door. You're friendly and approachable. You like to go with the flow and don't feel the need to be overly aggressive with patrons. You're naturally curious and constantly observing jungle behavior, but far from judgmental. You don't take things too seriously, but you are selective about who gets to see your inner savage. Whether on the main floor or back in the VIP area, you're the type to give a patron a GFE (Girlfriend Experience) without even knowing it. That's how cool and relatable you are. You can have a great conversation or you can just chill and be patient as the patron gradually falls in lust with your comforting aura.

If you are able to seamlessly combine and interchange these five personas—applying them at will—then you can reach the highest level attainable:

The Chameleon. Within seconds, you can switch from a calculated Seducer to an energetic Party Animal to an untouchable Celebrity to a talkative Therapist, and then casually smile and become the Girl-Next-Door. Simultaneously blending and camouflaging into any conversation, at any location, regardless of the temperature of the environment. Armed with a sharp tongue and extraordinary vision, you can be who you want, whenever you need to be, whenever you see fit.

A chameleon looking into a mirror sees a mirror.

—Unknown

STAGE 3: WHAT TYPE OF JUNGLE ARE YOU ENTERING?

It is vital that you know the advantages and disadvantages of your Home Club or any other jungle that you plan to enter. Many of you are so devoted to the club's brand name that you're reluctant to critique and thoroughly analyze the very place that forces you to pay a house fee. When you have an extremely slow night, it's easy to get emotional and overlook glaring issues that are staring you right in the face. Are you a pole assassin working at a club that doesn't appreciate pole gymnastics? Are you expecting a hip-hop mogul to come through and make it rain in a club that's known for 2 for 1 specials? Be realistic with your expectations. You must do your due diligence and always stay loyal to your agenda and not the club's. Self-perseveration is the first law of nature. Never ever forget the brand that you're working for: [**Insert Stage Name Here**]. When bills need to be paid and rent is due, you can't afford to miss any minor detail that will affect your bag.

Now, there are millions of jungles with playful names and fickle reputations (some seedy,

117

some respectable), that provide money-making opportunities for so many exotic dancers. Although some major establishments have managed to stand above and beyond the rest—case in point, there's no need to compare your neighborhood strip joint to the legendary and fortress-like Spearmint Rhino in Las Vegas. Come on, be nice! Look at the broader picture.

With close examination, there are four main types of jungles that you have to strategically navigate and have the foresight to see where **the money is flowing** (currently and for the future).

Where applicable, feel free to add in the particulars: Fully nude, Alcohol, BYOB, private parties, Bachelor parties, Bachelorette parties, After Hours, Champagne Rooms, Cigar Lounges, Special Events, Porn Star Features, etc.

The Traditional Club/The Franchise Club. This type of jungle is the cornerstone of the entire industry. These are the Cheetahs, Spearmint Rhino's, and Déjà Vu's of the world. And rightfully so, they are household names for survivors and for those who suffer from PTSD. At these clubs, you are the main attraction and the money flows around intimate conversation and lap dances (also stage and table dances). Whether fully nude or topless, the spotlight is placed precisely on a table where you and a patron can interact and play a game of strip club chess. Even though you have to deal with a costly house fee and tip out, you can butter your bread by serving up lap dances and therapy sessions in a booth or champagne room.

ADVANTAGES

- More one-on-one contact gives you a greater opportunity to create a solid client base (Regulars).
- Less distractions (television sets, sports games and rappers hosting) allows for more centralized focus on the main attraction—you.
- Sugar Daddies and Whales love to set up shop and take advantage of the discrete atmosphere.
- A strong brand name with stability makes it an easy choice for a Home Club.
- More VIP room action.
- Patrons aren't allowed to use their camera phones to record and capture footage.
- For most parts, waitresses and bartenders stay in their lane and stick to their job description—meaning the spotlight is always on you.
- Businessmen with quiet money like to creep into these establishments.
- More specialized events centered around you.

DISADVANTAGES

- You can be a small fish in a big pond.
- You can experience slow days, especially during the Day-Shift.
- They can afford to charge a higher house fee and tip out.
- They enforce more strict rules that may limit your hustle and creativity.
- Pickier hiring practices (looks, size, thickness, tattoos, experience, permits, licenses, background checks).
- More dancers means more competition.
- Less of a hip-hop vibe limits your chance for major rainstorms.
- They have total control over their marketing and social media campaigns.

OBSERVATION. Even traditional clubs are slowly but surely trying to reinvent the wheel. They are constantly looking for new ways to attract patrons, regardless to whether those patrons are strip club investors or not. They just want the traffic. Whether that means expanding their brand into more mainstream outlets like sports marketing or adding more sexy women to their street teams, the bigger they get, the more concerned they will be for their bottom line. Don't be surprised if you see more spectacles like cage matches, guest DJs, and UFC fights—even an increase in hosted events. Some establishments are even experimenting with Comedy Nights. Are you serious? They are also trying to expand the role of their waitresses, posting them on social media and encouraging them to set up thirst traps. Soon, there will be monthly Waitress Bikini Contests and other events centered around them—and not you.

As this type of club evolves and expands, there are two main questions you must always ask yourself:

Where is the spotlight going?
Are you still the main attraction?

Side note: Just know, if robot strippers ever become a thing, the traditional clubs will be the ones to introduce them to the masses. Talk about betrayal at the highest order.

The Topless Sports Bar/The Topless Club. This type of jungle is a mix between a sports bar and a strip club. A place where buffalo wings and lap dances are specialties on the menu. As you make your rounds, you have to watch patrons just as closely as they are watching the ballgame. In this jungle, the money flows around brief chitchats, restaurant style-food, and happy hour drinks—the dessert is you. But you still have to be extremely opportunistic and make sure that you take center stage when it's halftime. That's when you have to take advantage and remind patrons that you are *the only real game in town*. The energy in the room is high, the place is packed but this type of club forces you to play a game within a game. Money is definitely in the room, but you have to find the strip club fanatic and avoid the sports fanatic—there's a big difference.

ADVANTAGES

- You still have one-on-one contact that gives you a great opportunity to create a solid customer base (Regulars).
- Sustainable business, sports isn't going anywhere.
- Reasonable charge for house fee and tip out.
- Drink and food specials.
- Overall, sports fans bring a cool vibe.
- Lap dances and VIP rooms are still promoted.
- Patrons aren't allowed to use their camera phones to record or capture footage.
- For most parts, waitresses and bartenders stay in their lane and stick to their job description.
- Open hiring practices.
- Sports fans love post-game celebrations, and that's where you come in.
- Because of televised sports games and happy

hour specials, Day-Shifts can be busier than most.

DISADVANTAGES

- You can find yourself waiting for a patron to finish watching the sports games before engaging.
- Less hardcore strip club fans means less real investors.
- Sometimes you have to act like a sports fan when you're not one.
- A big group of sports fans, do not always translate to a bigger bag.
- Given the sports bar atmosphere and the drink specials, bartenders may receive more lustful attention and tips.
- Special sporting events (Super Bowl, UFC, Pay-Per-View Boxing) do not always bring more investors, but more spectators.
- Sports games are a natural distraction.
- You can get caught up watching a good game, forgetting about your agenda.

OBSERVATION. The more this type of club promotes their buffalo wings, happy hour specials and how many big screen TVs they have, the more they will condition their patrons to treat their establishment as a full-blown sports bar. You will find yourself hustling harder for the bare minimum.

Being topless will be forgotten and overshadowed by the intensity of a Game 6 playoff game. All you have to do is follow the thirst. If the thirst for sports is greater than the thirst for the half-naked dancers walking around, then you know the money flow in the room is stagnant. Don't be surprised if you start making less money than the waitresses. The fact is, you're already in a club that provides patrons with so many distractions. If you didn't know, there's only a few things that can compete with T and A— and that's the NBA, NFL, MLB, NHL, NCAA, and so on. When you find yourself waiting for the game to finish before you attack a table of patrons, then you know your animal ambition has been defeated.

As this type of club continues to promote every sports event on television besides its exotic dancers, there is one question you must ask yourself:

Is it time to work at a *real* strip club?

The Exotic Club/The Urban Club. This type of jungle is all about creating the hip-hop video experience and you're the video vixen (circa 2000s). Once the DJ drops a certified strip club banger, the lines between a strip club and a nightclub are blurred like the eyes of a baller on his second bottle of Henny. This is where the "movies" take place; the stage is lit, bottle sparklers are the main prop, and you have to audition for the lead actress in this ongoing movie series called "Secure the Bag." Why? The competition for money is a free-for-all. It's hidden in VIP tables, stacked in rubber bands, and safeguarded by hustlers and drug dealers. Money is also pouring down on the stage, creating a rainstorm that floods the floor. A few lap dances are still happening in the dark, but these patrons are after one thing; the spotlight. Rappers, athletes, and rainmakers all want to be seen. Even bartenders and waitresses find themselves joining the party and occasionally twerking for dollars. Things can get tricky in this club, and this is why some exotic dancers call it "The Trap."

ADVANTAGES

- You still have one-on-one contact with patrons, giving you a great opportunity to create a solid customer base (Regulars).
- Groups of female patrons periodically support you and your brand.
- Perfect party atmosphere for Nigh-Shift dancers who miss the nightclub life.
- All eyes can be on you.
- Reasonable charge for house fee and tip out.
- Networking opportunities to market your brand and acquire strip club fame that you can leverage for other business endeavors.
- Athletes, rappers and celebrities love to set up shop, and spread the wealth around.

- While on stage, rainmakers like to create thunderstorms, overflowing your bag with rain.
- This is where the "movies" happen.
- Video vixen and modeling opportunities.
- Parties hosted by socialites and celebrities provide the potential for a big payday.
- They play all the strip club anthems.
- The "movie" atmosphere makes it a fun choice for a Home Club.

DISADVANTAGES

- You can find yourself fighting for attention that is rightfully yours.
- Some clubs promote their waitresses and bartenders more than their dancers.
- Competition on stage and on the main floor for ballers can be intense and cutthroat.
- Not every athlete, rapper and celebrity who makes a cameo comes to blow a check on *you*.
- Unless for some popular lunch special, a scheduled appointment, or special event, Day-Shifts are rarely compared to the busyness of the Night-Shift (lowers income opportunities)
- House fee and tip out can jump up during special events.
- A booked table doesn't always translate to

more drinks and a bigger bag.

- Some patrons specifically come to see the person hosting, and not to invest.
- The nightclub vibe brings out more Spectators and Pretenders.
- Less lap dance and VIP room action (lowers your profit margin).
- Less hardcore strip club fans means less real investors.
- Too much camera phone usage and some patrons have an infatuation with taking selfies.
- Some clubs encourage their waitresses and bartenders to work outside their job description and twerk for dollars, emulating the skills and traits of an exotic dancer, instead of having them focusing on strip club hospitality.

OBSERVATION. Given the competition for these clubs to always attract the trendier patron who wants to book a table and get bottle service to achieve a particular look, the more these clubs will trend towards the nightclub vibe. How does that affect you? Well, in a nightclub, the main attraction is the attendee. It's all about them. Transferring that type of patron into a strip club environment does not enhance your game nor increase your bag. Of course, you might get a few drops of rain here and there, but to them, you're just an addition to the party; there's nothing exotic about you. You're on the same level as a go-go dancer. That outlook lends serious doubt to the use of the term "strip club culture."

And if you observe closely, you can see the signs. With more attention being placed on waitresses, bartenders, the person hosting, the guest DJ, the rainmakers, and everyone else who's glued to their cell phones taking selfies, you will slowly, if not already, lose the spotlight. At some clubs, you've already been eclipsed by the waitresses and bartenders. The money is flowing in their direction. The club doesn't mind because they are only concerned with their bottom line.

As this type of club evolves and expands, there are a few questions you must ask yourself:

Do you work at a nightclub that happens to invite exotic dancers? Or do you work at the strip club that gets so lit, that a party breaks out? Who's the main attraction? Are you just one of many? Are you on the same level as a twerking bartender or a flirty waitress ? If so, why are you paying a house fee?

The Local Club/The Hole in The Wall. This is the small-town club located on the outskirts of civilization. It's usually hidden in the dark, far away from suburbia (zoning laws), and normally close to an old landmark. It has a vintage marquee sign that screams that they were in business before Yelp reviews were a thing. Their marketing plans consist of a strong word of mouth. And you can tell by the customer base—local, traditional, and reliable. Just because it's considered a hole in the wall, doesn't mean the patrons have holes in their pockets. In this jungle, you are the one and only attraction. The spotlight is on you, and all eyes on are on the stage —exactly, where they should be.

ADVANTAGES

- Club is made for one-on-one contact that gives you a great opportunity to create a solid customer base (Regulars).
- You are the main attraction.
- Very reasonable charge for house fee and tip out.
- Lap dance and VIP action are the main attraction.
- Cheap drinks and food specials.
- Managers and staff can have a family business vibe.
- Patrons aren't allowed to use their camera phones to record or capture footage.
- This type of jungle puts the "Home" in Home Club.
- You can be a big fish in a small pond.
- Open hiring practices.

- Club rules can be lenient
- Locals are born Regulars.

DISADVANTAGES

- Don't expect to see a lot of athletes, rappers and celebrities coming through to blow a check.
- Special events don't seem so special when the same customers always frequent the club.
- Day-Shift can be a ghost town.
- The whole town can know your business.
- Open hiring practices (no standards).
- Sometimes management is shadier, and backroom politics are the norm.
- Less traffic means less possibility for thunderstorms and Sugar Daddies.
- Blue light shoppers and locals never feel the need to overspend.
- Being a big fish in a small pond doesn't always help your skills and game. Your typical strategy and predatory tactics might not fare too well in a big city strip club.
- Too much monotony and routine could drain your stripper spirit.

OBSERVATION. Unless this type of club plans on investing a bunch of money on expensive upgrades, in hopes of trying to ride the coattails of more mainstream strip clubs, the local club will continue to be a staple in the industry. In fact, as other clubs try to redefine the strip club experience with bells and whistles (television sets, hookah, expansive food menus), this establishment will become more of a destination because it sticks to the script. The club keeps the spotlight on its dancers.

As this type of club continues to focus on the *real* entertainment, there is only one question you must ask yourself:

Do you need to travel or bounce around for additional income?

DANCER NOTE

You gotta get in where you fit in. In an industry full of Sapphires and Diamonds, you'll never be the only dancer on a roll call. You have to quickly figure out what you bring to the table, how you maximize those skills and find a niche that you can exploit.

LAW
10

KNOW THE LINE

Morality, like art, means drawing a line someplace.

—Oscar Wilde

Rules. Every jungle has them. Some are extremely helpful to your money-making agenda, providing you with a relatively safe working environment to collect heavy rain. While others hinder your hunting skills and aim to tame that inner tiger from within.

But before you abide by any rules set by a club and assimilate into their corporate (or local club) culture, you first have to decide what works for you. What are your rules? What are you comfortable doing? Where do you draw the line?

Every single dancer has a line. They either:

Tiptoe around it.
Back away from it.
Or willingly cross it.

It's the stone-cold truth. In fact, depending on the patron, that line can turn into a curve or a figure eight over a span of two songs. It happens.

All is fair in lust and lap dances.

You'd be naive to think that every patron is treated the same. With the wide variety of characters that enter a strip club, equal treatment doesn't exist. The line is always drawn someplace.

The question is, where will you draw yours?

First, here's a bit of stripper wisdom that sums up this law perfectly:

What's good for the (Pink) Pony is not always good for the (Spearmint) Rhino.

The quicker you realize that only you control *your* actions, and focus on what's good for you and your methods, the quicker you can take care of your agenda.

There's only one law of the jungle—eat or be eaten.

And how are you going to eat if you're too busy watching other dancers devour their prey? Worrying and complaining about their moral code is an ongoing distraction that impedes your goals of securing a bag. You can't spend your time pocket watching and chaperoning another dancer's hustle. You're not a supervisor and you're not the eye in the sky.

Keep your eyes on the prize and your heels on the main floor.

Every step you take in the jungle should be direct and decisive. You can't claim to be a lioness and then stumble around cluelessly like a deer in the headlights. Be assertive and let your sharp teeth and stiletto nails (claws) show. Hesitation can lead to costly mistakes and a compromising of one's morality. In the powerful words of American politician, Shirley Chisholm: "When morality comes up against profit, it is seldom that profit loses."

Look into the mirror and quickly recognize what type of animal you are and where you will draw the line, in or even outside the jungle.

When it comes to your do's and don'ts—or maybes, there are few touchy topics that need to be addressed immediately.

You don't want to deal with any blurred lines.

FULL NUDE OR TOPLESS. Are you ready to put the "show" in showgirls? This is a decision that must be made from the jump. Before you submit an application, you should already know if you're comfortable walking around in your Birthday suit, free as a bird, in front of strangers—ready to spread your wings. Or are you only comfortable letting your nipples breathe so they can enjoy the lustful atmosphere? This is a monumental decision! Crucial. Your decision determines the type of jungle, the type of patron, the type of performance, the type of money, and the challenges that you may encounter on a daily basis.

LAP DANCES. For starters, are you afraid of touch? Do you completely understand its divine power and necessity? If you think a pat on the back can lift a patron's spirits, imagine their response from a satisfying lap dance. That cheesy smile is from ear to ear. Or do you cringe at the very thought of giving a total stranger a sensual, seductive 2 for 1 special? These are things you need to think about. Of course, you can you learn on the job. But deep down inside, you already know what you can handle. Be honest with yourself. Are you a grinder? Aggressive? Passive? Seductive? Shy? A pincher? A biter? A dominatrix? A therapist? A masseuse? Where do you draw the line?

Truth be told, a lap dance is where you

make your bread and butter. It's an easy way to capture any type of prey that comes across your territory. With the slightest of moves, you can give a patron PTSD or have him suffering from VIP Stockholm Syndrome. That all translates to a bigger bag.

Side note: If you're the type of dancer that prefers to give air dances, do not complain if that well runs dry. You know exactly what you're doing.

DATING PATRONS. Talk about a taboo subject. Immediately, some dancers will emphatically say, "Never date a patron. Period. End of story." But the truth is, it happens—regardless of the intentions of the meet and greet, outside the club—not only does it happen, a good amount of dancers will never admit that they use the jungle as a dating pool. When one is always hustling and doesn't have much of a social life, guess what? The jungle becomes more than a place of work. It becomes a social spot. The point is, if this is a line that you are willing to cross, then you have to be realistic. Understand the challenges and the type of investment that is needed to make a *real* connection. Because you are rolling the dice. You can meet some great guys or some wolves in sheep's clothing. Or you can meet some sexy girls or some she-devils. Whatever your preference, just know this topic will come up.

RELATIONSHIPS. This is where your maturity

and lady-like discipline are put to the test. Can you maintain a healthy relationship with a boyfriend or girlfriend while dancing? It's definitely easier said than done. Things can always start off on a good note. Rules and boundaries are established, and at the center of that discussion is a bond glued together by trust. But one slip of the tongue or an innocent mistake can open up a world of jealousy and deceit. Next thing you know, you're hiding out in the dressing room, playing a game of hide and seek with your ex.

This is why a lot of dancers prefer to be single. There's no guilty conscience and no need to report their racy activity back to a significant other. It takes a lot of weight off one's shoulders.

What about being married? Can you give a patron a mind-blowing lap dance and return home after the shift and get back to married life like nothing happened? Or can you rise above the madness and have a Bonnie & Clyde type of relationship? You know, where the both of you look at the jungle as a bank waiting to get robbed. If you can have that type of teamwork, kudos to that.

DRINKING. What's your limit? Do you know how much alcohol your body can take? Do you have the discipline and the mental fortitude to call it quits after your fourth tequila shot? When the bottles are popping and you're invited to a table, can you stick to your personal goals and request a boring ass bottled water? Can you do that? Can you handle the peer pressure or the heat of the moment? The one thing you can never do is be a lightweight who tries to keep up with a table full of alcoholics. You will enter a dark territory, and at the end of that tunnel is a killer hangover and a throbbing headache. You have to know when to draw the line. Forget money, your survival is at stake.

BACHELOR/PRIVATE PARTIES. Are you willing to entertain a group of savages outside of the jungle? Do you have an issue with going into the dark, trusting your stripper intuition and getting a different type of bag? A bag that doesn't require you to pay a house fee and tip out. It's all profit. Do you have a trusted partner that can vouch for the party and its undisclosed members? Do you know an ex-football player turned bouncer that can stand guard and wait for the code word, so he can bust down the door and wreckshop? Or are you 'about that life', showing up with just you and your outfits? This is definitely a line that you should already know if you're willing to cross it. If you think the strip club environment is unpredictable, then performing at a bachelor/private party full of drunken strangers defines the term, "element of surprise." And although the money may be good (or counterfeit), you will be reminded instantly that you're not in the jungle anymore. Especially, when you encounter the different types of animal behavior.

COMMUNICATION WITH PATRONS. Can you handle a bunch of strip club followers flooding your DM with daily schedule requests? Do you plan on being active on social media, posting photoshoots and twerk videos, advertising your brand and services? You know what comes with that, right? More DMs and, sadly, unwarranted dick pics. Will you be giving out your phone number (real or burner)? Do you plan on having a cell phone full of funny nicknames, so you identify your Regulars one by one? These are decisions that you need to contemplate. Without an agenda, you can feel like a customer service professional working at a call center, juggling all these busy lines and off-the-wall questions. Or you can stay off the radar. A lot of dancers like to keep a healthy separation from the jungle and their everyday life. They create a wall and keep communication with patrons (only Regulars and Sugar Daddies) to a minimum. The jungle is their office, and that's the only place they take their phone calls and meetings.

OBSERVATION. Having your own line doesn't mean that the profession lacks an overall value system. There are parameters that you have to work within to be an exotic dancer. This law is not about being lawless and a renegade to the unspoken rules (stripper etiquette) that dancers share amongst each other.

- If a dancer is already sitting at a table, engaged with a patron, that's not the right time for you to interrupt their conversation and try to snatch away her target. That's not having your own line or moral code; that's just being reckless and tacky.
- Borrowing a dancer's favorite lipstick and taking months to return it has nothing to do with self-preservation and being totally focused on your agenda; that's just inconsiderate and flaky.
- Telling beautiful lies and finessing a thirsty patron out of a large sum of money is a part of the game. But feigning sadness and telling that patron that you need to go VIP so you can pay the medical bills for your dying family member is a line that no one should cross. It's called the Art of Finesse, not the Art of Scamming.

DANCER NOTE

Before you abide by any club's rules that facilitate or hinder your game, you first have to establish your rules and what lines you are willing to tiptoe around, back away from, or cross. That way, you avoid hesitation and indecisiveness.

LAW
11

KILL THEM WITH KINDNESS

Don't mistake my kindness for weakness.

—Unknown

This law is not about navigating the savagery on the main floor and killing your prey with a warm smile and kind words. This law is about navigating and dealing with the sharks on the business side of the jungle.

As an exotic dancer, you must be aware of your partnering position in relation to the club and your place within the industry as a whole. Although you are the main attraction, the true mover, and shaker, the one who can be awarded the title

"Showgirl of the Month", or better, "Entertainer of the Year", you're still not in a contractual position to be given the award for the "Employee of the Month."

There are no certificates for you.

So, right off the bat, you know exactly where you stand.

You hold a different but unique place in the hierarchy of adult entertainment. You are the freaky freelancer, the traveling saleswoman, the part-time therapist, the crafty consultant, the entertainment—you are the independent contractor.

You work for you.

You're reminded of this every time you pay a house fee and tip out. And given that you have to abide by the club's strict rules like an employee, but you're not subject to their interpretation of the Common Law rules on what determines employee status, you can find yourself feeling overextended and in a constant state of limbo. It's a reflection of your volatility in the strip club game.

If you want to entertain a legal discussion on whether you're an employee or an independent contractor, or if you like being part of a small group that receives a paycheck, by all means pursue your goals, but you have to be honest. If you're a true go-getter, you enjoy the flexibility of being an independent contractor. You have the freedom to roam the jungle and hunt at any given moment.

That's a lioness.

This law is rooted in that independent stripper spirit.

Unless you plan on hitting the bachelor party circuit or opening your own sexually oriented business (SOB), you have to deal with the fact that you need the platform. What's an exotic dancer without a stage?

You're a partner—just not a 50-50 partner.

So, how you carry yourself and maneuver through the industry is crucial to your success. How do you handle disagreements? Because not everything will go your way. Your reputation precedes you as you continue to work at your Home Club and when you decide to bounce from jungle to jungle. The industry is relatively small. Words travel. You can't go around starting fires and burning bridges everywhere you go. You're a brand and that's not good for business.

You also can't let yourself be exploited, demeaned and treated like your services are not worthy of respect. Working with certain staff members and managers can be extremely challenging and disheartening. Some owners may reduce you to a piece of meat. You may face a corporate culture that practices colorism and workplace discrimination. As stated in Law 1, nothing is above an environment that's vehemently driven by the *bottom* line.

This is where killing them with kindness comes in.

Knowledge
Information
Nobility
Due diligence
Networking
Earnest
Skill
Success

Kindness does not mean weakness or softness. It does mean acting cowardly or passive. Kindness is knowing your worth and not succumbing to the expectations of how you are supposed to react to adversity in the jungle. When you face a serious challenge, you have to be ready to go in for the kill.

Kill them with **K**nowledge.

Thoroughly know the game you are playing. Observe, read, and soak up the strip club game like a sponge. Learn the ins and outs of the industry and your rights as a performer. But more importantly, know what's *right* for you and your brand. As an independent contractor, it behooves you to be able to gather pertinent information, store it away in your bag and apply it to your agenda whenever necessary.

Kill them with Information.

Valuable information is priceless, and that's why it's not easy to get. And there's a big difference between gossip and information. Gossip is hearsay and often riddled with fallacies. Good information comes from a reliable source and it's always pertinent to your current situation. You only want to retrieve information that can truly help your agenda. Anything else leads to confusion.

Kill them with Nobility.

No matter what obstacle you face, always stay classy and ladylike. Never let a club or staff take you out of character. Maintain your honor and moral integrity. It is strength. Becoming the stereotypical psycho, unstable stripper with emotional problems does not help your position as you navigate through the industry and face challenges.

Kill them with Due diligence.

Before you make a drastic move or take a major step to advance your dancing career, always do your research, do the math and put in the work before you make your move. When it comes to your business, you can't half-ass or half-step. You're an independent contractor; so that means you are the chief executive officer (CEO), the chief operations officer (COO), the chief financial officer (CFO), and the chief marketing officer (CMO) of your brand. Every move you make must be smart and well-thought out.

Kill them with **N**etworking. Being an independent contractor does not mean you need to be isolated and stuck in the jungle all by yourself. Branch out and network with dancers from different locations and clubs. Ask questions, bounce off ideas, and share information. Find a stripper consultant, join a support group, and learn from the OD's that have been in the game. But be genuine because no one wants to link up with a scammer. As far as clubs go, market your brand and let them know that you have skills, a strong following, and Regulars ready to support your cause. You're a business woman—you don't burn bridges, you help build them.

Kill them with **E**arnest. For whatever career move or moral position you need to take to better your career, always be purposeful and serious about your business. When you have a clear agenda, there's no time for immaturity and silly behavior. You are a professional and every decision you make must be direct and impactful to your brand. Stand firm and believe in your movement.

Kill them with **S**kill. Be good at what you do. Bring something to the table. When you transform into your stage name, have some substance and versatility behind your name. Work to be a "Jane of all Trades." Keep some tricks up your sleeve. Always be looking to improve your skill set. Make sure your stripper money cycle is in constant rotation. Like the popular saying goes, "Skills pay the bills."

Kill them with **S**uccess. Success is leverage. No club wants to lose a bonafide money maker. And if they risk it, don't fret, you can take your success, your Regulars, and your bag somewhere else. Nothing can stop your grind, and although it takes work and sacrifice, you will be a success wherever you go. And that success builds your confidence, strengthens your hustle, and enhances your game. Lastly, it also increases your bank account, allowing you to reinvest that money into your short-term and long-term goals.

DANCER NOTE

No matter what obstacles you face, never let anyone or a club take you out of character and put you in an inferior position. You're a business woman; you don't kill them with rudeness. You kill them with kindness.

LAW
12

AVOID GOSSIP AT ALL COSTS

Gossip needn't be false to be evil - there's a lot of truth that shouldn't be passed around.

—Frank A. Clark

This law is about a topic that is unfortunately on the tip of a lot of dancer's tongues: **Gossip**.

For millions of people, gossip is the new national pastime, gladly replacing baseball and football. With the advent of social media, the tea market has boomed with several outlets like TMZ and The Shade Room, supplying a thirsty public with something interesting to sip on daily. Millions are infatuated with sorting through people's dirty laundry and finding the latest tea to spill on their favorite celebrity and public figure. And some dancers can't help but to bring that infatuation inside the jungle, albeit with a different target in mind—you.

It's true that the environment provides enough dirt and grapevines to captivate a dressing room full of eager listeners. It's a jungle, and with all the masks, stage names and personas that move in and out, it's not hard to find a story to tell and a secret to expose.

Being that most dancers look at gossip as a form of entertainment, it's easy to get caught up listening to juicy rumors without regard to people's feelings and motives. Some consider it a harmless way to kill time and cure boredom, similar to flipping through channels, trying to find something amusing to watch on television.

But at its core, gossip is toxic and dangerous.

You can spill the latest tea, not knowing that it's actually gasoline that can start a fire in the dressing room, which can spread quickly to the main floor with no end in sight. Hearsay and she-said-she-said can create a noticeable tension that can divide an entire club with everyone taking sides in a stripper civil war. It can make coming to work an emotional challenge. The type of drama that starts catfights and brawls reminiscent of GLOW wrestling in the late 80s. A situation that can spill into the parking lot and online to social media accounts.

Back in the biblical days, gossip was useful for obtaining relevant information, hence the phrase "a little bird told me"—but in today's society and mainly inside your one and only sanctuary, those birds are buzzards carrying messages with the sole purpose of distorting the truth and rearranging facts under the guise of girl talk.

Do not encourage it.

As a professional, you should always display a certain level of tact and decorum. Especially in a tense environment where dancers are extremely sensitive about their appearance, status and ranking. There's absolutely no need to push buttons that don't need to be pushed.

Words are powerful and, more often than not, they are misinterpreted and taken out of context—unintentionally. In addition, sometimes "it's not what you say, but how you say it." A compliment to one dancer could be an insult to another. Gossip adds more fuel to that fire by adding words that are *meant* to belittle and demean one's stripper spirit. One rumor, no matter how outlandish, can damage a reputation overnight.

That's why you have to be careful with whom you share your secrets and intimate dealings. You can leave yourself open to lies and slander. And rival dancers revel at an opportunity to use your information against you, seeking to tarnish your brand and character.

This sentiment is tried-and-true—if a particular dancer will spread malicious rumors behind the back of another, she'll surely do it to you. It's just a matter of time.

If you reveal your secrets to the wind, you should not blame the wind for revealing them to the trees.

—Kahlil Gibran

You can't be surprised. To a gossiper, there are no boundaries and no topic is off limits. Whether behind your back or on full display in front of you and others, your secrets will come to light. And don't have a fallout with that dancer either as things can get really ugly.

The fact is that most people don't live by a code and gossipers only believe in the code of gossip —the juicier the story, the better! That's what they do. It's just girl talk, right?

Always protect your brand.

It's better to be closed-lipped than loose-lipped.

You may think that you're capable of ignoring lies and rumors, looking into the mirror and telling yourself: A lioness doesn't concern herself with the opinions of sheep.

But when they're directed at you and you've become the main attraction, but in a different way, those words will chip away at your pride and force you to defend your reputation. Given the circumstances, that can be honorable but in the grand scheme of things, it's a distraction from your agenda. While you're focused on the BS, money is heading in the opposite direction.

Foolishness doesn't pay the bills.

When it comes to gossip, take advice from the three wise monkeys that stay in the trees, sipping on bubbly, and observing the jungle.

SEE NO GOSSIP, HEAR NO GOSSIP, SPEAK NO GOSSIP

Avoid it at all costs.

You got money to make, and not gossip to entertain.

DANCER NOTE

Gossip is dangerous. It creates a toxic work environment that can severely distract you from your agenda. Instead of watching money going into your bag, you're too busy watching your back from dancers who are looking to start drama or settle it.

LAW
13

KEEP YOUR CIRCLE SMALL

Know yourself; keep your circle tight. Keep your friends and your work circle tight.

—Rita Ora

This law tackles the importance of establishing a tight-knit circle of friends that align with your moral code and stripper etiquette; a circle with no squares inside. Because when you're winning and getting to that bag, jealousy and envy take on ferocious levels. By the same token, vanity and cattiness rear their ugly heads.

But why?

For starters, if one has to deal with those

emotions in the concrete jungle, why should life in the lion's den be any different?

It's certainly not. The strip club is far from a utopia. It's a microcosm of the real world— animalistic, capitalistic, and socially cutthroat.

Especially when you consider the fact that you have to work alongside a distinct group of dancers from all walks of life; some with different religions, ideologies, and socio-economic backgrounds. Everyone is stuck in the dark fighting over the same men—talking about George Washington, Abraham Lincoln, Alexander Hamilton, Andrew Jackson, Ulysses S. Grant, and the ladies' man, Benjamin Franklin (even Thomas Jefferson is sought after, but he's often MIA). Everyone is also fighting for the same territory; a VIP booth, a velvet couch, or a celebrity's private table. You're bound to rub shoulders with some scammers, cat burglars, gossipers, backstabbers, and purebred hustlers. Face it, drama is inevitable.

The fact is that you're not working for the FBI. Most clubs rarely do extensive background checks and administer behavioral tests to see if dancers can mentally and emotionally handle the environment. They don't have proven ways to evaluate one's character and integrity. A psychologist is not on site to discuss one's deep-rooted views on sexuality and their proposed role in the hierarchy of adult entertainment.

Not every dancer is mature enough to be a

professional, and just because one has a clean criminal record, it doesn't mean that they don't have criminal tendencies—most cat burglars have a clean record.

For most parts, if you can turn a few heads and make a patron salivate from thirst, then you can get hired as an exotic dancer—it's that simple. And once you submit the necessary documents (permits and licenses), the application process is as elementary as saying the two letters, T and A.

Only months down the line, after a dancer has shown signs of shadiness and recklessness, will a club consider running a checklist and reinforcing the club's rules.

But for you, you have to watch your back and your front.

Patron's aren't the only savages.

With every exotic dancer driven by self-interest and their pressing agenda—along with the desire to stack money (tons of it) and to naturally compete for that money, it should come as no surprise that emotions run high, dancers get salty and feelings do get hurt.

It's part of the game.

Getting turned down by a patron and then watching that same patron walk off into the dark with your #1 hater can strike a nerve—even for a nanosecond. Although often concealed, petty questions are raised and innocent and catty judgements are passed under one's breath.

What the hell is he thinking?
He must like those type of girls.
She's not even cute.
How is that girl making money?
She must be doing something extra.

Every dancer is guilty. And because of the
nature of the environment, the hard truth is that
true friendship is a relationship that rarely gets the
time to develop and properly foster. It can definitely
happen, you can have a tight-knit circle but you
must have a mature outlook on the realities of the
job and environment. When you're dealing with
stage names, alter-egos and agendas, and the influx
of self-centered dancers flowing in and out the
jungle, most social interactions end up being on the
surface and quite shallow. It's not an indictment on
strippers and their character; the shallowness comes
with the territory. It's work, and the clock is ticking.

Given that time is money and it's also a
limited resource, you have to choose your circle of
friends wisely and exercise discernment. Be cordial,
ladylike and respectful to others, but be careful of
looking for a shoulder to cry on in the jungle. Unless
you have the best House Mom in the land, you'll
leave yourself open to a world of disappointment.
Simply put, not every dancer is capable of providing
emotional support and the right amount of
patience, loyalty, and honesty to sustain a bond of

friendship in a strip club.

As a professional—a businesswoman—you can't afford to waste time dealing with anyone's jealousy and envy, or any other type of catty conflict that can distract you from your purpose. Avoid gossipers at all costs and leave the scamming and the backstabbing behavior for the vultures and buzzards. Negative relationships, of any sorts, especially those disguised as friendships, drain you mentally and physically. Energy that could be harnessed and directed towards your agenda. You have to be so focused on your bag that if need be, you can go at it alone and not say a single word to anyone willing to stand in your way and bring you down.

If you cannot find a good companion to walk with,
walk alone, like an elephant roaming
the jungle. It is better to be alone than to be with
those who will hinder your progress.

—Buddha

And no one, absolutely no one should hinder your progress. Self-preservation is the first law of nature and you're an independent contractor— keyword: *independent*. But at the same time, you have to acknowledge that when you're working in a social environment, no dancer is an island. Naturally, there will be times where you'll want to team up to double up. Whether on stage or the main floor, hunting in a pack (The magic number of 3 or the power of 2) can help you secure a bigger bag. Again, that's why you have to be very selective with who becomes a part of your inner circle.

Your circle should have a common ethos. A common thread that binds you dancers together; a similar moral code and stripper etiquette. Not only is your circle aware of the 21 laws, but you respect the laws and their necessity. Your circle should be a protection from haters and distractors, not one full of them. Your circle must be able to appreciate what each member brings to the table—that's your strength. Unless you have an identical twin or you're a triplet with similar personalities and the same level of aggression, there will be a natural hierarchy within your circle—embrace it. The glue of your circle must be more than the ability to make money together. That's just the perk.

But if you build a circle based around shallowness and superficiality, that's when things can get real *funny style*. Some dancers constantly play favorites, only trying to associate and link up with those that can give them the right "look" and stripper status.

- A baller can walk into the club and request a group of dancers to his table. Moments later, you see your two friends from your circle downing tequila shots and laughing it up in the heavy rain. You're stuck on the side without a raincoat wondering why you didn't get the red alert signal.

- A dancer that's part of your circle can acquire a Sugar Daddy and quickly forget all about the sugary advice that you gave her that helped her land one. She now looks down on you from her pedestal and questions your purpose and status in the jungle.
- A friend can take a sabbatical and return with a new set of boobs and a new attitude. Just months ago, you two were stage partners, doing pole tricks and collecting rain. But now she has a "new body, new me" type attitude with a new agenda to match. She wants to speed up the money-making process and exit the jungle ahead of schedule. Translation: she wants to enter a new circle that will boost her stripper status and get her in front of athletes and celebrities.
- A close friend in your circle can switch up on you and join another clique overnight. She's now telling your business and gossiping to dancers that she knows you don't get along with.

As stated above, things can get real funny style. It's just another reminder of why it's called the jungle. Keep your circle small.

DANCER NOTE

Never forget that the same game that dancers can run on patrons, can be run on you. Keep your circle small, avoid drama and stay focused on securing that bag.

LAW
14

RESPECT THE THIRST

You should not see the desert simply as some faraway place of little rain. There are many forms of thirst.

—William Langewiesche

In *The 21 Laws of Surviving a Gentlemen's Club* —Law 16: Respect The Hustle, was a clear message about the importance of having a healthy outlook on the dancer's profession. This law is about the respect that you should have for the patron's thirst for your profession.

Thirst is a word that has many connotations, depending on when and where you use it. A male friend of yours can exhibit thirsty behavior with the ladies at a popular bar known for its single scene, and you can clown him and label him as gameless.

However, tell your close friend, who's standing in line with you at a packed nightclub, flirting with a bouncer, that she's acting thirsty and she'll automatically become defensive and self-conscious—and later on, irate.

After a long hike at Runyon Canyon, under the blazing sun, you and your girls decide to have a race to the water fountain. You quickly find your second wind and blaze past them like an Olympic track star because you were dying of thirst.

But in the jungle, *thirst* is a word that has a deeper meaning. Thirst is the main ingredient; it's the oxygen filling the atmosphere. It gives life and breeds prosperity throughout the environment. It represents an overflowing fountain of lust from which patrons can't stop drinking. It symbolizes an eternal flame placed in the darkness of a VIP room that will burn indefinitely. It continuously pumps blood into the heart of the multibillion-dollar strip club industry. It encompasses the desire, the yearning, the eagerness, the appetite, the craving, the lust. It's all about the **THIRST**.

Can you imagine if patrons didn't have

The
Hasty
Instinctual
Reaction to
Sexual
Tantalization?

Where would the industry be? Would there even be a strip club?

And you know this is true.

Be honest. You don't walk onto the main floor expecting an audience of religious monks who want to discuss the lifelong benefits of green tea and tip you with prayer beads and tea leaves. You also don't care for any patron who comes inside the club to disrespect you and act like a complete asshole. But you do expect the thirst, and you know that without it, there is no tip rail, no VIPs, no Regulars, and no bag to secure.

Thirst precedes the money; it is the horse before the cart. That's why this law is essential to understanding the scope of your profession.

To respect the thirst is to ultimately respect the game.

What helps you pay your bills? What keeps

the room packed with patrons ready to invest in your brand? What makes a Sugar Daddy bring out his sugar packets? What makes a Whale spout out his cash? What makes the lap dance the holy grail for Survivors? And what makes a young patron hit the ATM so he can make the rigorous climb up the patron's hierarchy of needs?

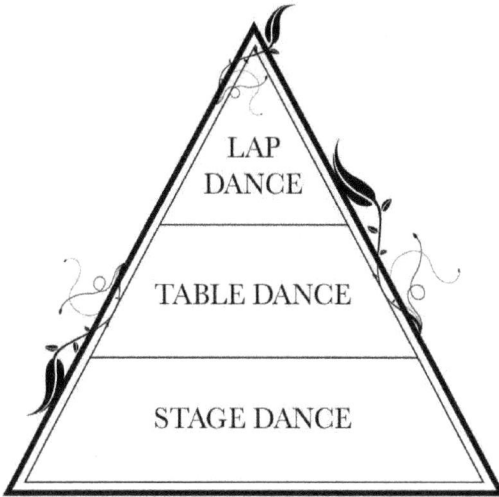

Fig. 1. Patron's Hierarchy of Needs.
From *The 21 Laws of Surviving a Gentlemen's Club* (p. 4), 2017, Varsity Club Publishing.

It's the **THIRST**.

And if discouraged and disrespected, the vital resource that provides so much life can easily go to another form of adult entertainment; Pornhub, cam girls, adult magazines, premium and private social media accounts, nightclubs, bars, and maybe in the future—Robot Strippers?!

It's imperative that you welcome the thirst, because if it leaves you wondering what happened and how you are going to survive the current drought, or worse, a recession, then *you* will become, of all words, thirsty.

Talk about irony?

The reality is that if you want a patron to respect your hustle, you have to respect their thirst. It's the yin and yang relationship. The same way it makes no sense for a patron to pay a cover and enter the jungle to spend their time demeaning you and talking down on your profession. It doesn't make sense for you to work in a lustful environment such as a strip club and be repulsed by a patron's thirst and appetite for T and A. Some dancers have a severe problem with masculine energy and its integral position within the game—in essence, disrespecting the game.

They spend the majority of their time belittling and detesting the very person who provides the majority of the money flow. That action is not only counter-productive to one's agenda, but it rips at the core of the primary union that supports the vitality of the entire industry.

Do not let your ego or your personal issues cloud you from addressing these simple questions:

What's an exotic dancer without a patron? And vice versa?

Just like there is no strip club without the stripper, there is no strip club without the patron. Period! Respect the thirst and your hustle will be respected and rewarded. Guaranteed.

DANCER NOTE

The unquenchable thirst for T and A is what provides life and prosperity for every single exotic dancer in the game. Disrespect the thirst, and the strip club industry will truly become a desert of destitution.

LAW
15

APPRECIATE YOUR REGULARS

*You should appreciate what you have, before it
becomes what you had.*

—Unknown

The **Regular**. The other half of the sacred
union that provides the foundation for the entire
strip club industry. The Regular and the Favorite
represent the yin and yang relationship that
symbolizes the oneness of the jungle. It's a match
made in strip club heaven. Both complimentary
sides get what they want (companionship,
compensation, freaky fun, reciprocity, relaxation,
and familiarity) and the establishment gets to

operate as a true strip club and keep their lights on.

There are several types of patrons that enter the jungle and invest on the daily, but none like a trusted Regular. They stand above and beyond the rest. Especially if you work in a club that's always full of civilians, casual-walk ins, Spectators, and Pretenders. Patrons that are just looking for a party, a sports game or a place to ogle over a sexy body and babysit a drink. Those types of patrons rarely invest heavily in your brand and, quite frankly, they don't help foster the core relationship that carries the entire strip club industry—the Regular and the Favorite. Once the party stops, or the ballgame ends, those patrons will gladly bunny hop to the next spectacle, looking for the next location to feed their need for the spotlight or personal time. It's about them—not you. But when the dust settles, the Regular, the true-blue patron will be at a table in the corner with a cocktail waiting for *you* to take a seat with no shenanigans—no cell phone, no sneak pictures and no intentions of exposing the details of your strip club engagement.

They are strictly there for you!!! Team [Insert Stage Name Here] all the way!!!

The Regular carries that burden and shows their loyalty to you and the fact that the exotic dancer is the main attraction, and when appreciated, they can provide you with something that is very rare in the jungle. In an environment that is naturally unstable and unpredictable, they can bring you stability.

For example, if you have three Regulars that you can count on to visit you at your Home Club once a month, and on each appointment, they spend an average dollar amount; a figure that you can roughly estimate given your past encounters. You can actually calculate a monthly budget and have a more precise plan of attack when it comes to achieving your short-term and long-term goals. That's why:

ONE QUALITY REGULAR IS WORTH MORE THAN A LARGE QUANTITY OF PENNY PINCHERS

Truly understand what it means to have a Regular. The dirty secret is that most dancers don't even have one reliable client they can call on in a moment of stripper crisis. They love to act as if they can go into their cell phones and send one flirty text message with emojis, and have a familiar face show up at the club like a knight in shining armor, but they are lying to themselves and to you. They can only hope to try to capture whatever fish happens to come into their net. This is the real reason a lot of dancers struggle to survive in the jungle. Rather than focus on their stripper money cycle and fine-tune their skills, they'd rather complain about the patron instead of learning the patron and understanding the game.

They mask the fact that they don't have Regulars by posturing and calling patrons names like tricks, pathetic losers, or any other comical titles (behind closed doors) that are intended to devalue the patron's vital position in the jungle.

Don't fall for it.

Whenever you hear a dancer ranting about patrons (not referring to those who deserve it), basically overcompensating for her lack of finesse and stripper spirit, immediately ask her this simple question:

How many Regulars do they have?

Look closely at her eyes as she struggles to find an answer.

Why?

Because the answer is zero. She doesn't have one at all. And there's no need to even think about her having a Sugar Daddy. You can tell by the bitterness in her voice that she hasn't had any sugar in her diet.

But dancers that have Regulars are too busy enjoying the benefits (monetarily and emotionally) to go on tirades. Favorites know that no patron is a better confidence booster than a loyal Regular.

When it's your birthday, and the Holidays, that's when a Regular shows up and shows out. When tax season hits, your Regular is right there ready to reinvest that money back into your brand. They are fully committed to your hustle and cause.

And when a drought hits and every dancer

who was bragging a month ago about their bag are now dying of dehydration and seriously thinking about jumping ship to a new club, guess who comes in the door with a smile, some flowers, and a nice bag?

Your Regular.

And truth be told, that's standard behavior when a Regular has a Favorite. But if you're lucky enough to earn the title of ATF (All-Time Favorite), then the world is yours.

Understand dearly that being anointed a patron's ATF is one of the most crowning achievements in the jungle.

Do not take that position for granted. No matter how highly you think of yourself as a dancer, and what you think you deserve, appreciate the fact that out of thousands of dancers across the nation, you were chosen as the All-Time Favorite. Although that achievement does not come with a bust trophy or a retired jersey in the rafters of the strip club, it does come with a steady cash flow and perks at your disposal. Believe that.

DANCER NOTE

Appreciate your Regulars. They provide stability, steady business, and brand loyalty like no other. They are crucial to the sustainability of the entire strip club industry. Put some respect on their names.

LAW
16

UPHOLD THE HIERARCHY

This law is an open reminder to solidify your high-ranking position within the hierarchy of the strip club. It has been mentioned several times throughout this book that **you are the main attraction**. A declaration that is unapologetic, and according to strip club gospel (Lap Dance 2:41), it was divinely etched in stone by the Stripper Gods. This lawful and just stance is a pro-exotic dancer—no ifs, ands, or buts about it.

It's all about you, your brand and your bag. Period.

Many may consider that declaration to be too traditional or archaic, or not progressive enough for establishments that want to mirror nightclubs and others that push the sports bar/strip club business model. But that doesn't mean those five words are false and somehow invalid. In fact, it's not only the stone-cold truth, but that declaration also holds the master key to maintaining a thriving strip club industry. One that feels the need to reinvent the wheel and constantly add bells and whistles, going away from its main source: the exotic dancer.

You are 'the entertainment'—the star of the show, not the person hosting, not the DJ, not the size of the big screen, not the Buffalo wings, not the happy hour specials, not the twerking bartender and waitress and certainly not some flavored hookah.

You are the one on the main stage, posing triumphantly at the top of the mountain, holding a golden pole underneath the grace and the benevolence of the Stripper Gods.

If the industry takes care of the exotic dancer, the game will take care of itself.

But as the industry evolves and becomes more mainstream, attracting a wider audience of patrons who might not know any better, or frankly don't care about order and rank—you must hold strong in your predominant position as 'the entertainment' and uphold the hierarchy inside the jungle.

Let's be honest, patrons don't pay a cover to see the DJ and to hang out with bouncers. The **THIRST** is for the exotic dancers. It would seem obvious, right?

Who puts the "strip" in strip club?
Who puts the "show" in showgirls?
Who are the gentlemen in the club coming to see?

However, in some clubs, you don't know who's the main attraction and that doesn't fare well for the dancer—financially and for future career sustainability. The lines are blurred and things that should be common sense are now becoming not so common.

Rappers are now looking to invade the strip club and take over the main stage, conveniently using the dancer as an extra. Socialites and Celebrities are coming to get their bag, and Unicorns (Porn Stars) dip in and out as they please. Patrons are trying to find ways to jump on stage and get their twerk on. And a whole list of entertainers (comedians, singers, bands, etc.) are plotting their way to get inside the strip club and occupy the stage.

Everyone wants the spotlight—*your* spotlight in the jungle. Entertainment is entertainment. But there's a big difference between an opening act and a headliner.

For exotic dancers, it's important to re-establish everyone's position in relation to your status as the main attraction.

There is a natural hierarchy and it's based

around your talent. Since you are paying a house fee and tip out, it's important to know where your money is going. You're an investor, and what type of return are you getting back from your investment? You have to play your position but everyone else has to play theirs too. If not, either stand your ground or find a location that truly values and appreciates the main attraction.

THE PROMOTER: If the club has a promoter, then first and foremost, they should be promoting the dancers. Anything else goes against your agenda.

HYPE MAN: If you have a hype man, that's a clear signal that you're working at an exotic/urban club. Technically, you don't need one. It's a strip club. But if you have one, make sure they say your name right and they say it often.

RESTROOM ATTENDANT/VALET ATTENDANT: It's all about strip club hospitality. A well-taken care of patron is more likely to make a return visit to see the main attraction: the exotic dancer.

THE HOUSE MOM: A good house mom is an assistant, a resource, and a personal manager that helps you and other dancers achieve your agenda.

BOUNCERS: Your stage name is your mental wall, your first line of defense. But that's mental. Bouncers are your physical wall. They are *your* secret service. They must protect the main attraction by any means necessary.

THE DJ: The DJ is your #1 spokesperson. Not only do they keep the party going with comical one-liners and continually playing sexually charged-up music, but they should be endorsing your cause and promoting your money-making campaign called "Secure the Bag".

THE BARTENDER: They serve the drinks, so patrons are ready to serve the dancer. If the bartender wants to twerk and play both sides, then she can start paying a house fee and hit the VIP to give lap dances. Otherwise, she is in complete violation of the game.

THE WAITRESS: A good waitress is Jill, the little sister of Jane of the Jungle. As a one-two combo, she delivers exceptional service and hospitality that gets the patron warmed up to spend money and have an amazing strip club experience with their older sister Jane. If Jill wants to spend her time twerking and invading your lane, it's your duty to let her know she's getting too big for her britches. If she wants to dance, she can fill out an application just like everyone else.

THE HOSTESS: A good hostess makes sure that true investors are settled in and ready to enjoy the entertainment: the exotic dancer.

THE MANAGER: A good manager not only manages all the drama and the corporate stuff, but mainly, they *manage* to make sure the temperature of the jungle is conducive to a positive money flow that circulates around the exotic dancers.

HOME CLUB: Every salesperson, needs a location to set up shop and conduct business. A Home Club is just that. A storefront where reliable patrons (Regulars) can stop by and purchase your top product: a strip club fantasy. Make sure you pick a location that centers around your main product and not one that devalues your product and tosses it on the shelf, on the clearance rack.

As an exotic dancer, you have the responsibility to know your worth and to uphold your vital position in a game that needs you to survive and thrive.

DANCER NOTE

   Never forget that you are the main attraction —the Exotic Dancer. Not anyone else. You are the source; the bloodstream that runs through the strip club industry. Uphold your high-ranking position in the jungle and stand your ground.

LAW
17

TRAVEL TO EXPAND YOUR CUSTOMER BASE

Opportunity dances with those on the dance floor.

—Anonymous

Just like any growing business that has established a foothold in their territory and target market, there comes a time where you will think about ways to increase your bag and expand your brand to a wider audience. Every great enterprise has taken that risk to look for greener pastures and you know there are plenty of jungles with investors looking for the new dancer on the scene.

And quite frankly, you're a saleswoman; not

only are you selling a fantasy, you are a self-made brand and your commercial product is an entertainment package full of sexy surprises: [Insert Stage Name Here].

It's only smart to expand.

Now, of course, you can continue conquering your local jungle and stay content with being the big fish in a small pond.

Or, maybe you're fearful of being banished from your current club for jumping ship and dancing for a competitor—some clubs hold their dancers hostage and brand them like cattle.

The choice is yours.

The money is out there and it's waiting for you to grab it. It's never fun watching a gold rush take place in another city, while you're at your home club experiencing a drought. At that moment, your loyalty will be tested. Especially if it took some time for you to find your Home Club and you've been holding them down with blood, sweat, and tears.

But overall, you must always lookout for #1. Stay loyal to your agenda and if your territory is dry and hasn't seen a drizzle of rain in months—or maybe a year—have the courage to make a move and set up shop in another location—not around the corner either.

It's time to earn those frequent flyer miles and if you like road trips, it's time to calculate that car mileage. You are about to take your show on the road.

TRAVELING 101

- **Do your research:** Just like any road trip, learn about the city, the club, and its surrounding areas. What type of jungle are you entering? What is the house fee? The club rules? What's the tip out? What is the temperature of the environment?

- **Have the proper documentation:** Permits, passports, ID's, licenses and fees, etc. Most clubs do not work with pop-ups, no matter how fine you are or how many followers you have on social media.

- **Be professional:** Whether the experience is good or bad, you are representing your brand, your state, and your Home Club.

- **Budget:** Budget, budget, budget. It's a business trip, not a vacation splurge. You want to leave with a bag of money and not bags from shopping.

- **Network:** Not only network with management and staff, but make a connection with dancers. Create a bridge that can transport hefty bags from city to city.

Traveling has its (obvious) benefits. It's a breath of fresh air. You can secure a brand-new bag and expand your brand. You can add a new experience to a chapter in your jungle book. But it mainly gives you the opportunity to see how your game stacks up against other money-hungry dancers from other areas. You can gauge your level of hustle and soak up game from performers that you might have otherwise underestimated and overlooked. Wisely adding new weapons to your arsenal.

Truth be told, after a while, it's easy to run your Home Club when you're the only lioness in the den. The subtle tricks and beautiful lies that you run on locals on a nightly basis might not stand a chance in a more aggressive, cut to the chase environment. For example, finessing a patron in **Los Angeles** is not the same undertaking as finessing a patron in **Houston**. Whispering sweet nothings to a patron in **Atlanta** (Home of the Strip Club Veterans) is different from flirting and telling beautiful lies to a patron in **Phoenix**. Dealing with the intensity and the high-stakes of Las Vegas, the jungle of all jungles, can have you feeling relaxed and nonchalant in a strip club-friendly city like **Portland**. Giving a patron a seductive lap dance in **San Diego** doesn't have the same expectations of doing a 2 for 1 special in **Miami**.

Although **Thirst** is the common denominator, the way patrons go about quenching that thirst varies, depending on the club, city, and local rules. Every club has a different climate and temperature. Some patrons live for the savagery and lawlessness of their territory. Not every patron is a Survivor and a proponent of *The 21 Laws of Surviving a Gentlemen's Club.*

You can hit the main floor in a new city and experience a culture shock and suffer from home club sickness after just four songs.

That's why, when you do travel, make sure you leave your ego at home and plan your trip with a sound budget and realistic expectations. Unless you're hosting or feature dancing for a legitimate event that guarantees you a bag, don't expect a red carpet pulled out for your arrival. Residential dancers will not be throwing you a welcoming party. They are very territorial. Most don't like pop-ups (and Ringers) coming to their club to cash in and then 'skirt out' in the middle of the night, without paying their dues and respects to the ODs who made the club what it is.

Rub a dancer the wrong way and she'll tell her crew to squeeze you out and make it uncomfortable for you to work and earn a single dollar.

It's not uncommon to travel to another city, enter a jungle and fail to make enough money to cover your travel expenses. You had plans on making a killing, but you're only left with a bag full of regrets and hard lessons. The dirty secret is that most trips aren't that successful. No one wants to publicly admit that their trip was below expectation and, financially, they went into the red. But if you go by social media, every trip was a movie that needs a sequel, asap.

Whether traveling in a stripper entourage or on a solo mission, you have to be ready for anything and your eyes must be wide open. If you're willing to take the risk to travel, and if you can pull off a successful trip, the reward can set you up for months. You never know until you try. There are plenty of cities that provide enough jungles with opportunities for a new bag and look no further than the Tree of Life:

L.A.
OXNARD
SAN FRANCISCO
SANTA BARBARA
OKLAHOMA CITY, BOISE
JACKSONVILLE, CHARLOTTE
ANAHEIM, TAMPA, MIAMI, TULSA
LEXINGTON, SEATTLE, ORLANDO
DALLAS, DETROIT, CHICAGO, HOUSTON
PHOENIX, NEW ORLEANS, ATLANTA
CLEVELAND, BALTIMORE, MINNEAPOLIS
INDIANAPOLIS, NEW YORK, HONOLULU
FAYETTEVILLE, DENVER, LOUISVILLE
PORTLAND, EL PASO, RENO
NEWARK, PHILADELPHIA
TOLEDO, TUCSON
SAN DIEGO
AND
THE JUNGLE OF ALL JUNGLES,
LAS VEGAS

EVENTS

If you're serious about that bag, you should have a pulse on every single major event that happens in America. Especially the ones that bring a thirsty crowd looking for a lap dance and a cocktail. Your calendar should be filled with money-making events like the Super Bowl, the World Series, NBA All-Star Weekend, the NBA Finals, Daytona 500, the Final Four, Spring Training and both political conventions —Democrats and Republicans like VIP booths too. Don't forget about CES, the AVN Awards, BET Awards Weekend and Comic-Con—nerds also make it rain. The number of events are endless and wherever there is major rain and a strong money flow, you can be planning your trip to capitalize and expand your customer base.

DANCER NOTE

If you're 'about that life,' then traveling to expand your brand and your customer base is a no-brainer. Just make sure you're prepared to handle a new environment and be realistic about your expectations. There is no reward without risk.

LAW
18

FOCUS ON YOUR GOALS:
SHORT-TERM VS. LONG-TERM

What you get by achieving your goals is not as important as what you become by achieving your goals.

—Zig Ziglar

While you engage with patrons, telling beautiful lies and enhancing the fantasy, be careful not to get enamored by the *jungle's* fantasy and lose complete focus on your personal goals. The jungle has a seductive way of turning you into a donkey chasing a carrot on a stick. You'll be twerking your tail off to secure that ever-elusive bag; the type of payday that can have you riding off into the sunset. You'll start to recite so much scripted dialogue that you begin to lie to yourself and fall for the illusion that all that glitters is gold. You jokingly tell patrons about your plans to take courses at a local City College or at a prestigious university as if it was a legitimate joke to be told over and over again.

Slowly but surely, you forget that you have *real* life goals to accomplish.

Time flies, and you're not there to chase a carrot on a stick and grind for the glitter. You have a clear agenda and a purpose that goes beyond collecting $1 bills. Take in the following quote:

Money is a good servant but a bad master.

—Francis Bacon

Never let the jungle dangle the carrot in front of your face and lead you astray from what's important. Money is a tool and dancing is a means to an end. You can't be wandering aimlessly through the jungle without a torch, a self-made map or an escape route. You do have a life outside the strip club.

Your stage name is just that—a stage name.

Having short-term and long-term goals and knocking out those goals will help you maintain a healthy outlook as you adapt to the environment and keep your eyes on the prize. They also give you hope that you will not die hopelessly on the main floor or wither away on the pole.

No one dances forever.

You must always plan for the next chapter in your next book.

Whether working to be a registered nurse, starting a clothing line, obtaining a real estate license, or booking studio time for your fire mixtape, you have to be dead serious about your goals. Write them down. Make a vision board. Find the time to attack your goals like you do a simpleton on the main floor begging for a lap dance. In case you forgot, there's no tenure for dancers, no safety net, no 401k, no pension and no retirement plan. As an independent contractor, the onus is on you to take care of your brand and, ultimately, yourself.

#STRIPPERGOALS 101

Where applicable, feel free to add your short-term and long-term goals to the list. Everyone is different and goals are unique to the individual, but, overall, self-improvement and leveling up is the objective.

SHORT-TERM GOALS

- **Every dollar counts.** But it always feels good to hit your *target dollar amount* for your shift. Put in the work and keep your stripper money cycle in rotation.

- **Bills, Bills, Bills.** You gotta pay those bills —and pay them on time!!!
- **Treat yourself.** There's no love like self-love.
- **Tip yourself.** If you have to pay a tip out, shouldn't you tip yourself in the process?
- **Pay your car note, rent or mortgage.** Transportation and shelter are necessities.
- **Get that credit score right.** That's an important number that can allow you to maneuver through life and knock out some major goals. Ideally, you want your score to be 700 and up.
- **Finish that book, ace that course, get that certification.** You must always push forward with your education—mainly self-education.
- **Get out of debt.** Less debt means more financial freedom.
- **Drink more water.** Health is wealth.
- **Eat healthy.** Again, health is wealth.
- **Invest in your in brand.** If you're going to enter the jungle, you might as well play to win. That means promote, market, and build equity into your stripper brand.
- **Exercise.** Stay fit and ready for the main stage—essentially any stage in life.
- **Invest in your relationships.** Healthy relationships with family and friends push you to become the best version of yourself.

LONG-TERM GOALS

- **Slow money.** There's nothing wrong with investing your money on the side while you grind (mutual funds and stock portfolios). Don't be afraid to let your money bubble quietly.
- **Just as important as having a Regular, you must have a trusted CPA on your team**. You have to make your money work for you and not against you. That's the American way.
- **Are you planning on starting a business?** You have to be your own angel investor. Do you have up to two years of capital saved to keep your business afloat? Creating a sustainable business from the ground up is a tough challenge and you have to be ready to survive the ups and downs.
- **Travel.** Grab your passport, get away from the jungle and live a little.
- **Health care.** If you slip and fall off the pole, do you have health insurance or are you fitting the entire bill?
- **Earn that degree.** Knowledge is power.
- **Dental plan.** Fixing those pearly whites can get expensive. Do you have dental insurance?
- **Life Insurance.** A small payment a month

can go a long way to covering pricey funeral expenses.

- **Find a Home Club.** There's no place like home. If you plan on dancing for a few years, it's good to set up shop and find a home base for your brand.
- **Buy a house.** If you're serious about being a home owner, you better save up and make sure that credit score is in good standing.
- **Exit Date.** Hustle hard so you can pick an exit date and retire gracefully from the game.

Out of all the goals, the toughest one by far is the one that sounds the easiest—save your money. In a consumer-based society, you are groomed to spend it as soon as you get it. It's easy to read a meme that tells you to "stack your money and repeat", but to actually let it stack and accrue is sometimes mission impossible. That's the catch-22 when dealing with fast money. It comes and goes quicker than a tequila shot. You must dig deep— real deep and find the discipline to save for a **rainy day**.

Save a boyfriend for a rainy day - and another, in case it doesn't rain.

—Mae West

Jokes aside, it's not always going to be heavy rain in the jungle. There will be a time when a major drought will hit or life itself will simply throw you a monkey wrench and suck your bank account dry. You need to have money stored away for emergencies (personal and family). This goal is a no-brainer, but life in the fast lane doesn't encourage you to switch lanes and think bout the short-term and long-term consequences that come with life in general.

Every dollar counts and saving money for a rainy day is a goal that shouldn't be a milestone—it's a major part of your agenda.

DANCER NOTE

Securing the bag is not your only goal. Don't forget that money is a tool to be used to level up and improve your quality of life. Having short-term and long-term goals will help you stay the course and maximize your limited time the jungle.

LAW
19

WHAT HAPPENS IN THE JUNGLE,

STAYS IN THE JUNGLE

AND

WHAT HAPPENS IN VIP,

IS YOUR BUSINESS

*Be discreet in all things, and so render it
unnecessary to be mysterious.*

—Arthur Wellesley

The first half of this law is about discretion
—specifically social-media discretion.

For patrons who adhere to *The 21 Laws of Surviving a Gentlemen's Club*, exercising discretion is of utmost importance. It's not only an honorable trait, but it's also a strong reminder of why the term "adult entertainment" is used. An *adult* knows when it's appropriate and beneficial for them to close their mouth, stay in their lane and work within the guidelines of the game, thus respecting the game. They know that visiting a strip club is still a private affair, despite what a generation of misguided patrons and civilians believe. A lawful patron would never think of using their cell phone to record footage of you in action or take childish selfies as if one was gaining some type of credibility. They know it's essential to have a healthy respect for the hustle, the dancer (and her privacy) and for the privacy of others. They believe wholeheartedly that what happens in the jungle, stays in the jungle.

But what about the clubs?

The staple clubs like the Spearmint Rhino's and Déjà Vu's (and most of the topless sports bars) already understand the importance of discretion. These establishments have strict policies on the use of cell phones or any other recording devices inside the club. Just watch what happens when a drunk patron tries to take a selfie by the tip rail, during a dancer's showcase performance. He's quickly called out by the DJ for having terrible strip club etiquette and he's met by a WWF looking bouncer named Big John.

Situation handled.

The dancer's relieved and glad that her right to privacy was upheld, enforced and respected.

In these clubs, the boundaries and behavioral expectations have already been established and you can tell by their social media campaigns that they are relatively conservative and safe. They control the narrative, posting just enough to get the patron's attention to lure them inside— mainly weekly promotions, special events, party packages and thirst traps—knowing that the full strip club experience—discrete and private—can only start once they enter the green door. Some clubs do go a step further and post dimly lit twerk videos, and "go live" to show off their sexy waitresses and a few dancers on stage to deepen the trap—but even that is only a snippet—you can grab some kettle corn and that live stream video has already been cut short.

On the surface, dancers may want more freedom to advertise themselves on their club's platform and be part of their marketing plan beyond a real-time roll call or a headless butt shot, which they can do on their own personal accounts, but they understand the club's traditional stance and overall strategy. It's best to *leave something to the imagination.* And these clubs specialize in keeping the velvet curtain closed. They know that what happens in the jungle, should stay in the jungle.

But for dancers who particularly work at

exotic/urban clubs and smaller establishments that rely heavily on social media for their advertising, discretion is a dicey topic to discuss.

Considering the intense competition between clubs and the need to advertise their roster of dancers (some only promote their waitresses and bartenders), it's common to see the best twerk videos, tons of sexy (almost explicit) images and party flyers hyping up the next "movie" event. Those posts make total sense. The competition for business is intense and their target audience of Rainmakers and Ballers have a thirst for more and more content. And dancers at these clubs are also feeling the heat. Their social media accounts are lit with flirty videos and photoshoots slaying the gram and getting thousands of Likes on the daily, all with the purpose of letting their followers know, where they can book a table and have a great time with the dancer as the main attraction—but don't forget that bag.

However, what's in question is when some clubs post intimate pictures of patrons and dancers in the jungle, engaging and cavorting in what should be private behavior. Some things *are* best kept in the dark. Not only that, but some of these clubs allow their Spectators, Pretenders, and Civilians to stand and record the racy activity in the jungle with no shame or regard for the dancer's privacy and the privacy of others. Just tearing the velvet curtain back and ripping it to shreds. It's to the point where clubs might as well invite a film crew inside and do firsthand interviews while patrons are getting twerked on and putting singles in G-strings.

Why not?

It already seems that discretion has been tossed aside for foolishness in the name of marketing.

Some dancers are okay with this exposure, using it to their advantage and taking out their own cell phones and recording life in the jungle. It's their choice. But overall, it's a slippery slope for dancers and the game as a whole.

Where does it stop?

Does anything stay in the jungle? Is there such thing as privacy?

Regardless of the club, every single dancer should know the line when it comes to social media and the amount of exposure one is willing to tolerate or readily release.

It is still an open question, however, as to what extent exposure really injures a performer.

—Harry Houdini

Houdini, the great magician and illusionist, was talking about the dangers of exposing the secrets behind his magic. What about your magic? Is it possible to expose too much?

You have to decide. Once a video or an image is in cyberspace, there's no getting it back.

If you see no issue with patrons recording you inside the club, then that's your M.O. But keep in mind that if you or other dancers in that particular club don't draw a line, then you can't expect patrons to draw one either. You are basically encouraging patrons to have a lack of code and, best believe, if you give an inch, an unlawful patron will always take a foot—and then leap across the line. Don't be surprised if they become more invasive and brash with cell phone usage. Some will certainly abuse it—paparazzi style. What's next? Will a patron pull out his cell phone during a lap dance, record it and make it go viral? Or maybe that's already happened. But you can't get mad since you never put your foot down. And you're the one who opened up the floodgates without considering future consequences.

If you're using social media for marketing purposes, make sure you have a solid plan and your campaign is effective. Take notes and see how many real investors you acquire from going live and flooding your timeline with selfies and thirsty captions. Just like a club, you have to look out for your bottom line. You want to promote your brand, pull in potential Regulars and not entertain a bunch of onlookers thirsting for a free show—which is inevitable on a public platform. The last thing you want is for your viewers to lose the incentive of going into the jungle and just settling for your twerk videos online, saving them a cover cost, tips, and stripper equity. Unless you consider making money on a premium site or from a paid subscription, that's the game you're playing. Remember: You set the *real* trap inside the jungle—not on social media.

In society, social media has been and will continue to be a game changer. How it further impacts the jungle and its inhabitants remains to be seen. Without a code, the strip club can completely lose its definition and never be the same. Then what happens in the jungle is for everyone's consumption. But as an exotic dancer, you should never forget the power of mystery.

The mystery is what prompted men to leave caves,
to come out of the womb of nature.

—Stephen Gardiner

If you're the type of dancer that prefers to stay off the radar and move in the shadows, hold fast with your decision. You are holding the game intact. To be elusive, unattainable and rarely seen has an allure that never fades. To give a patron an amazing strip club experience and then vanish back into the concrete jungle like a mythical creature is the stuff of strip club legend. One can post 1,000 twerk videos and 1 million selfies, but there is no better marketing strategy than word of mouth. Real money talks quietly and those discrete conversations are what bring out the hefty bags. What happens next, stays in the jungle.

WHAT ABOUT THE VIP ROOM?

Discretion is a necessity and, in the jungle, VIP doesn't only stand for Very Important Person, but it also stands Very Important Protocol. You're an adult and what you decide to do with your prey is up to you. They fell into *your* trap, not anyone else's.

If you want to give a Sugar Daddy or a Regular a high-mileage lap dance, or even worse, an air dance—that's your business. It's between you, the patron and the Stripper Gods.

But be careful. If you decide to be extra touchy and engage in a little extracurricular activity, don't forget that there are consequences to your actions. Whether it be the other eye in the sky, or a nosy bouncer on watch pushing the envelope and tiptoeing the line, or even crossing it, your reputation and income can be put in danger.

Every club has rules and they vary depending on the type of establishment and location; the town, city, county, and state. And they're governed by puritans that handle the often-hypocritical politics of that region. These puritans publicly shame the jungle, but secretly have a favorite couch in the VIP room of their go-to club —and a stripper on speed dial.

Therefore, you never know when the powers that be will try to rain on your parade—not the type of rain you're probably thinking about. It's best that you proceed with caution when handling your business—private and discreet—sipping on your tea, not spilling it. Stay fluid and be chameleon-like —moving through the jungle with stealth and camouflage—you are there one moment and gone the next.

Understand that the dark is your ally. In this environment, what happens in the dark doesn't have to come to light—unless you insist on telling your business. That's the *real* inner beauty of the jungle. In a room full of masks and stage names, not everything is meant to be revealed. Lawful patrons understand and respect discretion, and that feeling should be mutual. You wouldn't want a patron to put you on blast and expose your tricks of the trade. It's vital to embrace the dark and the importance of maintaining confidentiality.

You have the power and influence to keep things concealed and under wraps. You set the tone and draw the line. Just by the way you carry yourself, patrons will know that you respect discretion and maturity. You don't tolerate any childish behavior—this is "adult" entertainment.

What happens in the jungle, stays in the jungle.

If you're serious about your bag and agenda, then be discreet in all things. As a result, you keep things intimate and mysterious, which makes patrons come back and empty their pockets for more VIPs.

DANCER NOTE

Discretion is an asset that never depreciates. Without discretion, the jungle becomes an open playground full of foolishness and reckless behavior. An environment that loses its mystery and intrigue.

LAW
20

YOU ARE WHAT YOU EAT

Tell me what you eat and I'll tell you what you are.

—French Proverb

As stated numerous times throughout this book, there's only one law of the jungle—eat or be eaten. And while you survive and continue to adapt to your environment, you will eventually be confronted with one question: What are you eating?

As far as the typical strip club menu, you're already familiar with the appetizers: tasty patrons with open pockets, and the main course: hearty Regulars with seasoned bank accounts and the grand finale, the much anticipated, mouth-watering dessert: a sweet stack of Benjamin Franklins, sprinkled with George Washingtons.

The perfect reward to end a hard-earned meal.

With a steady diet, you can sustain a worthwhile career as an exotic dancer. But if you're not careful, your overall appetite can severely knock you off balance and, before you know it, your life is sinking into pit of quicksand—drowning deeper into a hole of decadence.

It's vital that you monitor your diet with mindfulness and discipline. Understand that the jungle breeds excess and gluttony—and if you over-consume the food that's in the jungle, you will surely become one with the jungle—chaotic and cannibalistic.

MONEY. Money makes the world go round, and inside the jungle, things are no different. You want it, you need it and it's floating around in the air waiting for you to grab it. Everyone knows why you're there. There's no hidden agenda. It's all about the money. But don't let the thoughts of making money consume you to the point where that's all you think about. Some of you wake up in the morning thinking about money, and every time you go to sleep, you're counting dollars instead of sheep. Right under your pillow is a brick of cash and below your bed is a box of trash bags. But don't forget that money is simply a tool. It shouldn't govern every move you make and determine how you treat those around you.

MAKE MONEY, DON'T LET THE MONEY MAKE YOU

There's more to life than counting money at the end of the night. You weren't born to be a slave to the dollar bill. And you surely didn't come out of the womb with a stage name and a pair of baby stilettos. You have other talents to offer the world besides knowing how to secure a bag. Make sure you keep a healthy perspective on what you're doing and why you're doing it. Never lose touch with the fact that money is a means to an end—not the end itself. If you do, you will always find yourself doing "something strange for a little change." No amount of money in the world is worth your soul, right?

LOOKS/COMPETITION. In the jungle where it is lawful to create a compelling visual, it is natural to be concerned with your looks and how you measure up to other dancers. Possessing the ability to turn heads is the difference between securing a bag or securing a mercy tip. Because of this never-ending battle for dollars, you can always catch a dancer in the mirror checking out her body and making sure that her appearance is on point. No dancer in their right mind wants to be a bottom feeder and the last

206

link in the stripper food chain. Behind every smile is a ruthless desire to "slay" the competition.

But if you become preoccupied and consumed by your competition, you will never feel confident in your looks and what you bring to the jungle. You'll constantly compare yourself to other dancers and end up chasing behind them instead of focusing on your skill set and your clients, inadvertently sabotaging your brand and turning your strengths into weaknesses. Sooner or later, you will contract a deadly flesh-eating disease that attacks your self-esteem and self-image. You'll literally start picking your body apart—nose, lips, boobs, hips, and ass. This dire need to reach bodily perfection will lead to irrational decisions like rushing to get butt injections from a fake doctor in a back alley; sadly to impress and one-up your competition who can really care less about your insecurities.

FOOD. The jungle is far from a farmer's market. Unless you work at a club in Portland that serves vegan food or you pack your own lunch, you'll be hard-pressed to find an abundance of fruit bowls and vegetable platters on a strip club menu. At best, you can eat a Caesar salad or nibble on some carrot and celery sticks with ranch, but how sexy is that? As far as snacks, don't expect any Trail mix as you wander your way through the jungle. However, you can go to the bar and settle for a bowl of salty Beer

Nuts. But overall, the only thing *organic* in the jungle is a patron's appetite for a curvy body.

Outside of a juicy T-bone steak and lobster tail, most clubs are a step above fast food restaurants. They offer up the following items: tacos, pizza, hamburgers, and Buffalo wings—definitely not the healthiest of selections, but damn good! Some clubs even tease you with breakfast and lunch buffets and dare you not to grab a plate and pig out. But if you're not watchful of your eating habits, you won't even notice the unwanted weight gain that can come out of nowhere and show up in the wrong places. When you're too busy being a party animal and overindulging on lemon pepper wings and french fries, it's tough to stop and think about your daily diet. Mix those greasy items with beer or your favorite cocktails and, over time, your overall health can take a plunge into a place of low self-esteem and sluggishness—qualities that do not help your mental and physical health.

ALCOHOL. As money flows, so does the alcohol—all types—cocktails, shots, champagne, beer and brown liquor. In a social environment full of party animals and lustful strangers, it's customary to break the ice with a drink. It's a welcoming gesture that relaxes both parties—you and the patron. Alcohol has long been proven to lower inhibitions and release a heavy dose of dopamine. Take a sip of your favorite cocktail and the flirting begins. The patron makes it rain, the DJ plays the hottest strip club anthems and the drinks keep coming. But this isn't about knowing your limit and drawing the line while you're having a good time during the encounter. Indeed, that's where the issues start. This is about your Total Alcohol Consumption (TAC). How much alcohol are you drinking in a day? A week? A month? A year? Is the jungle turning you into a closet alcoholic?

As much as you would love to be on a champagne diet, your body wasn't built to handle that type of lifestyle. Until clubs start selling smoothies or you have enough discipline to stick with bottled water, you have to monitor your alcohol intake. Not only is there nothing sexy about alcohol poisoning and vomiting in the dressing room, but you can spiral out of control and put yourself in situations that can have *real* consequences. It can be a matter of life and death.

And even if you happen to work at a jungle that has a juice bar—a club that does not serve alcohol—that doesn't mean you're totally off the hook. You can easily become addicted to energy drinks that can increase your blood pressure and cause insomnia. Not to mention dehydration which leads to real thirst and there's only one person that should be thirsty in this scenario: the patron.

MUSIC. What's better than a good strip club anthem? The right song can give you an adrenaline rush as you twerk up a storm and collect heavy rain. It awakens your inner savage. And while the beat is infectious and perfectly catered for twerking, the lyrics of the song won't be anything to brag about. You'll hear your share of "bitches and hoes" and the demands to "bust it open" and "show'em what you twerking wit." You know, the modern-day strip club soundtrack. Although you will hear words of encouragement, mainly about excessive drinking, doing drugs and turning up, there's no surprise that the lyrics represent the precarious nature of the jungle; capitalistic, carnal and self-indulgent.

It makes sense. You don't expect hear "How Will I Know" by Whitney Houston or "The Boy is Mine" by Brandy & Monica. But it's certainly not healthy to listen to strip club anthems 24/7. Being an exotic dancer is something you do—not who you are. You're multidimensional and when you leave the jungle, give yourself a mental break and listen to different music. Relax your mind with some 90's R&B, or soulful oldies from the 60's, or classical music—hell, country music.

Do you really need to wake up early in the morning, eat breakfast and hear a song about "poppin' molly" and "touching your toes"? Are you really trying to transform into "Diamond" while you're running errands and grabbing a coffee? Music is powerful and it communicates to your spirit. The rhythm and lyrics infiltrate your brain like alcohol infiltrates your bloodstream. It's good to detox every now and then from the "face down, ass up" choruses and listen to music that can alter and elevate your spirit. Songs that can tap into a different emotion and put you at peace, away from the intensity of the strip club life.

DRUGS. It's one thing to experiment, dabble or even fall victim to peer pressure, but it's another thing to find yourself in the parking lot popping pills, drinking lean or smoking weed to muster up enough courage to face the jungle. If you can't transform into your stage name without being high or sedated, then you should find another line of work. The jungle will eat you alive and spit you out. You should be able to rely on your natural instincts to hustle and the mental fortitude to handle an environment full of temptation.

A real professional can perform sober and make a killing. Being dependent on drugs is not a "good look" and if you let drugs consume you, they will take over your agenda. Before you know it, you'll be twerking to supply your cocaine addiction rather than twerking to better your future. Not only are you damaging your health, but drugs cloud your judgment and cause you to be out of touch with your stripper intuition. It's hard to listen to your stripper-sense when that tingling sensation is coming from a foreign substance and not your gut. Awareness is key and drugs do not keep you sharp and alert.

When you do find yourself off-balance and on the verge of losing your identity, give yourself time to step away and reexamine your appetite and diet. You never want to get to the point where you have difficulty distinguishing between your stage name and your everyday persona. As much as you would love to feed your ego, you can't be a savage 24/7/365. You must know when to be on the take —your personal TAKE.

Time Away Kick-starts Energy

TAKE FIVE
TAKE A BREAK
TAKE TIME OFF
TAKE A TIMEOUT
TAKE A BREATHER
TAKE A STEP BACK
TAKE A GIRL TRIP
TAKE A ROAD TRIP
TAKE A PEACEFUL HIKE
TAKE A MINI-VACATION
TAKE A LONG VACATION
TAKE UP A NEW HOBBY
TAKE UP MEDITATION
TAKE A YOGA CLASS
TAKE A PILATES CLASS
TAKE TIME AWAY FROM THE JUNGLE
BEFORE THE JUNGLE
TAKES YOU OVER

Your sanity and well-being are at stake. Do whatever you have to do to keep a healthy separation from the jungle and that starts with your diet. You are what you eat.

DANCER NOTE

It's one thing to work in the jungle, but it's another thing to *live and breathe* the jungle. Do not let the extremities of the strip club life consume you to the point where your mental and physical health affect your everyday life.

LAW
21

KNOW WHEN TO EXIT THE JUNGLE

The best time to start thinking about your retirement is before the boss does.

—Unknown

Similar to a world-class athlete that has spent tireless years in the spotlight mesmerizing fans and performing jaw-dropping feats, there will be a point in your career where you will eventually lose a step. Your skills on the pole suddenly diminish. Your lap dances fail to arouse and stimulate overspending. Mentally, you'd rather stay in the dressing room and read a book than hit the stage and deal with unruly patrons. Overnight, you become a shadow of your vaunted stage name. You wake up one day and stroll into work and face your ultimate adversary—not a drunk patron, not an asshole of a manager, and not a conniving stripper who wants to steal your Regulars—but the wall.

This meeting is inevitable.

You can deny it all you want, but it happens to every single dancer that's pulled up a G-string and strapped on a stiletto.

And if it hasn't already, at some point, it will happen to you.

The DJ grabs the microphone and announces your stage name to the crowd, "Coming up next to the main stage is a dancer so hot...that she can only go by one name...Fire!"

But sadly, you won't be able to bring the *heat*. Not even a spark; not even a flicker. Tip rail quickly turns into a ghost town as patrons quietly leave their seats and escape to the back of the room. The DJ tries his best to shame patrons into staying seated by throwing out one-liners, but it's too late. Nothing can be done. The only tips that you do receive are from your co-workers who want to give you an assist and make sure your self-esteem is still intact.

As that scenario plays on repeat and you experience a case of perpetual déjà vu, one day you'll return to the dressing room and pull up a chair. And just like a scary movie, out of nowhere, you'll see these words written on the wall:

EXIT THE JUNGLE

However, your ego and pride will get in the way. Although deep down inside, you know that you're dancing on borrowed time, it's tough to face reality and leave the strip club life. That's why, ideally, you should already have an exit strategy and a specific time you want to exit the jungle; one that is detailed and precise. As a professional, you should revel in the challenge of knocking down a major milestone, and what's bigger than retiring with a Santa Claus bag and smile, knowing that you mastered the game. So are you bold enough to sign your stage name on the dotted line? Go ahead and enter that date and time and make it official.

MONTH • DAY • YEAR   HOUR : MIN

_____

_____
[STAGE NAME]

But it's easier said than done. Most aren't strong enough to stick to their exit date and follow through on their decision to gracefully bow out. The jungle has a sinister way of interrupting things, toying with you, and initiating a game of tug of war. As soon as you think you have the upper hand, and one foot out the door, you'll get pulled back in with the promise of a bigger bag. The jungle is smart and persuasive; it knows that shit happens, bills pop-up, and family members need help. It knows that the hustler inside of you will always refuse to throw in the towel. You've been on the grind too long and you're obsessed with the paper chase. You love the adrenaline rush that comes from securing a bag. But just like gambling in a Las Vegas casino, you have to know when to cut your losses and the exit the premises before the sharks come.

Exotic dancing is a young woman's game. Even though you do have your share of MILFs that add diversity and experience to the stripper ecosystem—which is greatly applauded and respected—the point is, who wants to be on stage in their 50's doing the splits and wearing discontinued platforms? There's a reason why Amateur night exists. The jungle has a craving for new flesh. It's always about the "new dancer" on the scene. The key is to never let that night become a slap in the face.

Because, at some point, you will need to humble yourself and take heed of the signs. First, you'll start to stand out, but not in a good way. Instead of having an exotic quality that oozes sex appeal, the only thing you can command is sympathy—you become the queen of mercy tips. You lost your power to seduce. Unknowingly, taking on the role of the strip club sideshow. Early in your career, you could sense vulnerability and weakness in a patron, but now they look at you and smell uncertainty and desperation. On the main floor, your catwalk lacks swagger and persuasiveness. It's like watching a harem of zebras getting chased by a lion, and there's that one zebra that's lagging behind and everyone knows it's just a matter of time.

You simply turn away.

And that's exactly what patrons do. You can be a household name—Candy with the Double Ds who's been loyal to the same club for 10 years (30 in stripper years). But when your time is up, there will be a new Candy on the scene. A young dancer with Double Ds, a curvier ass, and a spunkier personality. All of a sudden, your Regulars start to have wandering eyes. They stop sliding into your DMs and inquiring about your schedule. More importantly, your bag gets lighter and lighter.

It's all part of the revolving door of the strip club industry. Surely, when you arrived on the scene and became a Favorite for thirsty patrons, that triggered the demise of another dancer who couldn't keep up. When she packed her bags and exited the jungle, you didn't shed a tear and throw a retirement party. You kept it moving. And that's how the game goes. It doesn't matter if you spent a pretty penny on plastic surgery or went out and bought a bunch of brand-new outfits. When the signs are there, it's best to make the decision before the jungle does. That way, you can exit the game on a high note, feeling accomplished and ready to explore a new environment. You did your time and you can close that final chapter in your jungle book.

As Jane of the jungle, there are three red flags that signal that you should strongly consider retiring from the game:

Money is not a clear motivator. If money doesn't motivate you, then you seriously have to question your purpose in the jungle. You don't come to work to chitchat and pass the time. The jungle is not your neighborhood coffee spot where you strike up a light conversation and take advantage of the free Wi-Fi. You're on the clock, and money is to be made. You can never lose your ambition to hustle.

That's like a lioness that can't find the right motivation to hunt for her pride. At that point, that lioness ceases to be a lion. The same goes for you. Money has to be the motive. When you're having a tough time dealing with patrons, staff and fellow dancers, at least you can always fall back and deal with the comfort of knowing that in your bag is money. The ends justify the means. But if you don't want the ends, then you're taking up space and valuable time for someone who's ready to eat.

Embracing rejection is too challenging. Can you imagine a salesperson that can't handle their emotions when losing a sale? What about an aspiring actress that gets irritated with the auditioning process? Exactly. You can't because certain dispositions come with the territory. To hustle is to be subject to rejection and having thick skin is a prerequisite. If you start to get extremely frustrated with every interaction and highly disappointed from a patron's decision to spend money on another dancer, then it's time to look for another hustle.

The jungle is a social environment that's purely capitalistic. When it comes to patrons, you win some and you lose some. Getting turned down shouldn't chip away at your soul and attack your self-worth. You can't function in the jungle if you're annoyed with the concept of customer service, asking a patron if they would like a lap dance and initiating a flirty conversation. Going from a social butterfly that is strategic and calculating to an apprehensive dancer who is tense and reluctant to put in the work is self-sabotaging and pointless.

Your mind wants to twerk, but your body doesn't. This factor gets overlooked. No one in the game wants to discuss aches and pains, and the occasional corns that pop up on your feet. It's simply not a sexy topic and it won't garner you any followers on social media. But if you're wearing knee pads, looking like an old roller-derby player from the 70s and every time you twerk, do a pole trick, or perform a lap dance, you need to take a breather and grab an energy drink—the writing is on the wall. It only goes downhill from there. First, it's the water in your knees and then the scoliosis in your back. Soreness moves up your spine to the top of your neck.

In your rookie years, your stage routine was your gym workout, but now you dread sliding down the pole. You try to do your signature move, but it doesn't have the same effect. You used to "make it clap"—but now you can only make it cramp! That's when you find yourself hiding out in the dressing room getting a muscle rubdown from your house mom. You're on the stripper injured reserve list and you don't even know it.

DANCER NOTE

You can't dance forever. Just like the dollar bills that you love counting, your days in the jungle are numbered. It's best to be honest with yourself and face the music when it's your time to leave the game.

STRIPPER MONEY CYCLE

SEX APPEAL DRAWS THEM IN…
HUSTLE KEEPS THEM ENGAGED…
GAME MAKES THEM COME BACK…

GLOSSARY

THE LANGUAGE OF THE JUNGLE

Knowing the language of the jungle is equivalent to knowing the sounds of the jungle—it keeps you alert, aware and on your toes. Being able to talk the talk, and walk the walk is a clear sign of a professional.

AIR DANCE: A non-contact lap dance where there is so much air between the patron and the dancer that the patron feels deflated and utterly exploited. Unlike a table dance or a stage dance where no contact is customary, an air dance is usually unexpected and unsettling. It is the absolute worst dance a patron can receive.

ASSIST: A tip given to a dancer on stage by another dancer, strictly for moral and financial support.

ATF: All-Time Favorite (See Favorite). The ATF is a term only reserved for a dancer who has reached the level of a jungle goddess.

BAIT AND SWITCH: The ploy of using a stack of cash (brick) as bait to attract dancers to a table, giving them the illusion of a big payday then switching up and only spending a small amount of cash.

BLUE LIGHT SHOPPER: A patron who purposely visits the jungle to babysit one drink and pray for 2 for 1 specials.

CAT BURGLAR: A dancer who is a petty thief. She is adept at stealing items in the dressing room and scrapping money on the stage (or main floor) that isn't hers.

CIVILIAN: The average woman who does not work in the jungle and likes to visit for fun.

CLIMATE CHANGE: A drastic change in the jungle that immediately affects a dancer's ability to operate and roam freely. These changes are attributed to a business decision made by management or enforced by local authorities.

CONCRETE JUNGLE: A general term used to describe the world outside the jungle. This world is also exploitative, capitalistic and predatory.

COUNT UP: The joyful event of counting up one's money at the end of a shift.

DOLLAR DIVING: An alarming scene where several dancers are aggressively snatching dollars off the main floor, creating a feeding frenzy that is cringe-worthy and startling.

DROUGHT: A period of time in the jungle where there is little cash flow and no chance of rain. Unlike stripper stagnation, a drought is usually due to external issues (Climate Change) and circumstances that are out of a dancer's control.

EXTRACURRICULAR ACTIVITY: Use your imagination.

FAVORITE: 1. A patron's favorite dancer. Although a patron may claim to have several, only one will receive the majority of the patron's resources (time and money). 2. A Favorite is one of the two halves of the lustful union that makes up the core foundation of the strip club industry. The powerful yin and yang relationship between a Favorite and a Regular provides the energy flow that supports the entire strip club industry.

FINESSE: To smooth talk your way into getting what you want with minimal effort.

FORCE FIELD: A dancer's natural barrier that is placed up to protect their government name, personal information, and private life.

GEORGE: A very generous tipper; as in George of the Jungle. The name refers to "George" Washington on the front of the coveted one dollar bill.

GFE: Girlfriend Experience. Not to be confused with the full-fledged definition used in the world of high-end escorts and call-girls. In the jungle, this term describes an intimate connection between a patron and a dancer that goes beyond the typical business interaction. A Favorite usually offers a Regular a Girlfriend Experience; long talks, neck massages, therapy sessions, warm hugs, an open ear, and a genuine concern for their well-being without the daily struggles of a girlfriend & boyfriend relationship.

GREEN CARPET TREATMENT: After a patron makes it rain, the floor or main stage becomes covered in cash, creating the appearance of a newly placed green carpet.

HOME CLUB: A dancer's favorite jungle to hunt; a primary residence for a dancer who prefers not to leap from jungle to jungle like a leopard.

HOUSE FEE: A fee that dancers pay to work in the jungle. Unlike employees, dancers are independent contractors who have to pay to take advantage of an atmosphere that provides the paying patrons.

JANE: A stripper, as in Jane of the Jungle.

JILL: A waitress; the little sister of Jane of the Jungle.

JUICE BAR: A jungle that doesn't serve alcohol.

JUNGLE: The appropriate name for a strip club. It represents the exploitative, capitalistic and predatory nature of the strip club environment.

JUNGLE JUICE: Any brown liquor.

THE JUNGLE OF ALL JUNGLES: Las Vegas.

LAP DANCE: An erotic, intimate, one-on-one dance in which a dancer sits, caresses, grazes or grinds a patron's lap for the duration of one song. Additional touching from both parties may take place based on the dancer, the shift, and the jungle. Tipping is optional.

THE MAGIC BROOM: When the stage is flooded with so much money that a bouncer has to grab a push broom and help sweep up the money. The appearance of the broom is a magical sign of prosperity.

MERCY TIP: A tip given to a dancer on stage purely out of sympathy because no other patron is tipping.

MILEAGE: A patron's term that represents the amount of physical contact and extracurricular activity that a patron can get away with during a lap dance.

MILF: An acronym for Mother I'd Like to Fuck. Inside the jungle, a MILF is an older woman in her dirty 30's and filthy 40's with a kid or a few, who is a seasoned veteran with many years of stripping experience.

MOVIE: A night or special event that was or will be so epic that you swear it had to be pulled out of a movie directed by one of Hollywood's masters of cinema.

NEWBIE: A young dancer who is learning the ropes and the environment.

OD: Original Dancer. A dancer who's been in the game for years and can tell you about the ins and outs of the life and all its perks and trappings. OD is a play on the term 'OG' (Original Gangster).

OUTSIDER: A civilian who is a staunch critic of dancers and the strip club industry.

THE PATRON'S HIERARCHY OF NEEDS: The motivational theory that everything flows and revolves around the three-level pyramid of services. The coveted lap dance is at the top of the hierarchy of needs, followed by the table dance and, lastly, the stage dance. The three levels enable the patron to utilize their five senses (sight, hearing, smell, touch, and taste) to their maximum.

PERVERT ROW: Another name for Tip Rail (See Tip Rail).

POLE ASSASSIN: A dancer who's an absolute beast when it comes to pole work.

POLE WORK: A dancer's artistic, high-flying, gymnastic performance on a shiny brass pole. Some dancers deserve gold medals for their Olympic pole working skills.

POP-UPS: Foreign or out-of-town dancers that pop-up out of nowhere, hoping to work at a popular club during a special event or weekend.

POST TRAUMATIC SPRUNG DISORDER (PTSD): A mental condition triggered by experiencing a strip club event so mind-blowing that the patron becomes sprung to the highest degree. The symptoms are chronic or acute.

RED ALERT: The welcoming signal that a notable baller or a whale has entered the jungle to spend a lot of money.

REGULAR: 1. A regular is a patron who frequents a jungle; a recognizable face that is familiar with the environment and its inhabitants. 2. Formerly considered a negative label (some consider being a Regular a pathetic loser), a Regular is one of the two halves of the lustful union that makes up the core foundation of the strip club industry. The powerful yin and yang relationship between a Favorite and a Regular provides the energy flow that supports the entire strip club industry.

RINGER: An experienced dancer who purposely visits a foreign jungle for Amateur Night, especially if there is a cash prize.

ROOKIE: A young, misguided and agenda-less patron who is naive to the ways of the jungle.

SABBATICAL: A hiatus, typically a few months, taken when a dancer gets plastic surgery.

SCAMMER: A dancer who specializes in scamming patrons with trickery, lies, thievery, and con games.

SCRAPING: The act of swiftly grabbing money on a crowded stage, ensuring that one stakes their claim.

SECURE A BAG: To obtain, secure or acquire an amount of money that will allow you to maintain a level of success, ensuring your survival in the jungle.

SIMPLETON: A foolish patron that lacks the common sense and awareness to understand that one's survival is at stake. This patron thinks everything is fun and games, and being economical is silly.

SPECTATOR: A patron who simply watches all the activity in the jungle with no plans of getting their hands dirty or spending money.

STAGE DANCER: A title that represents a dancer that prefers only to perform on stage. The use of this title is an indirect way of indicating to a patron that she is not a fan of giving lap dances.

STRIPPER EQUITY: The amount of interest (time and money) invested into a dancer with the expectation of return.

STRIPPER DARTS: An unflattering game where patrons crumple up dollar bills and throw them at dancers on stage as if their body was a dartboard.

STRIPPER GODS: The deities in the sky that look down and bestow blessings on dancers who are in dire need of good fortune and rain.

STRIPPER INTUITION: The quality and ability of a dancer to have keen insight and perception on an event, situation, or person in the jungle independent of any reasoning process.

THE STRIPPER MONEY CYCLE: The quality-based theory that every exotic dancer must possess three essential qualities to not only make money but to sustain a worthwhile career in the jungle (Sex Appeal, Hustle, and Game). This theory is represented by a circular model that shows the three qualities flowing in unison and creating a cycle around the core necessity: money.

STRIPPER STAGNATION: A prolonged period of time where all three phases of the stripper money cycle are in severe decline. This stagnation is usually due to laziness and unprofessionalism.

STRIPPER YEARS: Similar to dog years, a theory based on how the jungle and its intense environment ages a dancer faster than the normal experience gained with a typical job. The simple rule is to multiply the years of dancing by 3. Ex. 4 years of dancing is the equivalent of 12 years.

SUGAR DADDY: An older man (usually well-off) who financially sponsors a young woman's extravagant lifestyle in exchange for companionship.

SURVIVOR: A patron who thoroughly understands the 21 laws and adapts to any challenge in the jungle, regardless of the type of club and location. This patron knows the benefits of tipping, the importance of customer service and respects the dancer's hustle.

TARGET: A patron who's on a dancer's radar. The dancer is locked in and ready to engage.

THERAPY SESSION: The therapeutic listening session that happens in VIP between a dancer and a patron, where the dancer plays the role of the therapist and provides an open ear, a shoulder to cry on and sound advice.

TIGER STRIPES: A colorful and more appreciative term for stretch marks.

TIP OUT: A tip that most jungles require dancers to give employees, typically the DJ, bouncers, managers, and bartenders. Every jungle has different requirements.

TIP RAIL: The seating area around the stage where a patron can tip and admire the stage show. Historically, a tip was placed on a golden brass rail that served as a barrier between the patron and the exotic dancer.

THE TRAP: A more hip-hop influenced name for the jungle.

UNICORN: A porn star. Once in a blue moon, a porn star will make a magical appearance in the jungle.

V.I.P.: An alternative acronym that means Very Important Protocol. This acronym is a reminder of the importance of privacy and discretion when it comes to the activity in the VIP room.

VIP STOCKHOLM SYNDROME: A psychological phenomenon when a patron is lured into a VIP room and stuck in there for hours, getting fleeced for all their money and, somehow, the patron expresses extreme sympathy for the dancer and her economic plight. Despite the enormous amount of money spent, the patron feels the dancer got the raw deal.

WHALE: A patron who has deep enough pockets to swallow up a dancer and hold her hostage for several hours, especially in a VIP room.

X-RATED VISION: The ability of a dancer to see through a patron's pockets and spot their true intentions and purpose in the jungle.

INDEX

G

H

I

L

M

N

O

P

Patron's Hierarchy of Needs, 8, 9, 11, 164
pimp, 29, 70
porn stars, 30, 112, 118, 175
Portland, 183, 185, 207

Q

quicksand, 205

R

roleplay, 80
Runyon Canyon, 162

S

sexbots, 43
social media, 7, 16, 40, 43, 120, 121, 139, 148, 149, 164, 182, 185, 194, 196, 197, 198, 199, 200, 221
Spearmint Rhino, 118, 133, 195
Stripper Gods, 33, 39, 58, 62, 63, 110, 173, 174, 201
Stripper money cycle, 9, 10, 12, 13, 34, 77, 91, 94, 147, 169, 189
Sugar Daddy, 30, 36, 61, 77, 159, 164, 170, 201
Super Bowl, 123, 186

T

Tampa, 185
Thomas Jefferson, 90, 154
TMZ, 148

U

Ulysses S. Grant, 90, 154

W

weed, 211
WorldStarHipHop, 39

Y

Yelp, 129
YouTube, 33

Z

Zig Ziglar, 59, 187